'This is a chronicle of possibilities for U.S. workers and employers. Cobb's encyclopedic roadmap makes crystal clear what can and should be done. There is an international research-driven explosion of laws, codes, ordinances, and guides screaming that attention be paid to harmful psychosocial hazards (PSH) in workplaces. Numerous Occupational Health and Safety (OHS) agencies and professionals around the world are advocating for the inclusion of workers' psychological health in the list of employers' responsibilities, an expansion of the duty of care as currently practiced in the United States. Rather than targeting workers for fixing, the book details that much of the rest of the world focuses on how to identify and mitigate work environment problems that create psychological injuries to workers.

This wonderful book throws down the gauntlet to challenge the United States to follow the paths of Nordic countries, Ireland, Spain, the United Kingdom, Canada, Australia, Mexico, Japan, and developing countries, which have implemented ILO and ISO guidelines. The most innovative advances are attention to loneliness (United Kingdom), making return to work safer (South Australia), death from overwork (Japan), and a requisite disconnection from work outside work hours as enforced by several nations. Solutions do exist to take on the scourge of psychosocial hazards that are ignored in the United States. Will employers here voluntarily redesign work in response to the pandemic to align themselves with their international counterparts? This book refutes the proffered excuse that they could not know what to do.'

Gary Namie, Ph.D., *Co-founder and Director,*
Workplace Bullying Institute

'This is an incredibly rich primer for US organizations about the nature and seriousness of psychosocial hazards as a major occupational health and safety risk. Using clear and accessible language, Cobb makes the case for the elevation of psychosocial hazards as an even more powerful driver than the physical hazards of work-related stress and the impact on employee and thus organizational health and wellbeing. Grounded in an examination of prevention and mitigation approaches of a number of countries, Cobb identifies specific steps that US companies can and should take to help their employees, and thus their organizations, to thrive.'

Loraleigh Keashly Ph.D., *Professor, Communication;*
Associate Dean, Curricular and Student Affairs, College of
Fine, Performing and Communication Arts; Distinguished
Service Professor, Wayne State University

'Ellen Pinkos Cobb has built on her global comprehension of employment law and policy to offer a smart analysis of psychosocial hazards in the modern American workplace and how to respond to them. This welcome framing of health, mistreatment, and stress at work ultimately prevails upon U.S. employers to embrace a fuller duty of care for their workers. Especially when one adds COVID-19 to the "pre-existing conditions" confronting the world of work, this book arrives at an opportune time.'

David C. Yamada, *Professor of Law and Director,*
New Workplace Institute, Suffolk University
Law School, Boston, MA

Managing Psychosocial Hazards and Work-Related Stress in Today's Work Environment

Today's evolving world of work makes it imperative for employers to manage psychosocial hazards (PSH) and risks leading to work-related stress. This book contains essential, general, and country-specific information and templates for the successful management of hazards to prevent psychological harm in the workplace.

Acknowledged as global issues affecting all workers and industries, PSH are work factors that have the potential to lead to physical or psychological injury and stress, relating to how work is designed, organized, and managed, and to work relationships and interactions. This book advances the idea that management of PSH, and psychological health and safety, is part of the duty of care of today's responsible and ethical employers to employees, and that U.S. employers should recognize this responsibility. Clear and easy to follow, this guide presents comprehensive information on addressing PSH, discussing measures taken internationally (laws, guidance, and resources from Europe, Canada, Mexico, Australia, and Japan), and a new global standard on psychological health and safety at work. (Note: At times within this book, and Part II in particular, punctuation may be added to quoted provisions for ease of reading and for consistency.)

Practitioners and students in the fields of management, occupational health and safety, human resource management, ethics and compliance, occupational health psychology, and organizational psychology will come away with a deeper understanding of the importance of PSH and their management.

Ellen Pinkos Cobb is an attorney, author, and subject matter expert on international workplace bullying and harassment laws, with many years of experience working in the international occupational health and safety and U.S. employment discrimination areas. This book is her third with Routledge; she has previously published *International Sexual Harassment Laws for the Multinational Employer* (2020) and *Workplace Bullying* *and Harassment: New Developments in International Law* (2017). Much of this book was written as a 2020–2021 Visiting Researcher at Bentley University's Hoffman Center for Business Ethics.

Managing Psychosocial Hazards and Work-Related Stress in Today's Work Environment

International Insights for U.S. Organizations

Ellen Pinkos Cobb

Routledge
Taylor & Francis Group

NEW YORK AND LONDON

Cover image: © Brian A Jackson (Getty Images)

First published 2022
by Routledge
605 Third Avenue, New York, NY 10158

and by Routledge
4 Park Square, Milton Park, Abingdon, Oxon, OX14 4RN

Routledge is an imprint of the Taylor & Francis Group, an informa business

Library of Congress Cataloging-in-Publication Data
Names: Cobb, Ellen Pinkos, 1958– author.
Title: Managing psychosocial hazards and work-related stress in today's work environment : international insights for U.S. organizations / Ellen Pinkos Cobb.
Description: New York, NY : Routledge, 2022. |
Includes bibliographical references and index. |
Identifiers: LCCN 2021059870 | ISBN 9781032034508 (hbk) |
ISBN 9781032034485 (pbk) | ISBN 9781003187349 (ebk)
Subjects: LCSH: Job stress–United States. | Work–Psychological aspects. |
Work environment–Psychological aspects. | Occupational health services–United States. | Industrial safety–Psychological aspects.
Classification: LCC HF5548.85 .C63 2022 | DDC 158.7/2–dc23/eng/20220120
LC record available at https://lccn.loc.gov/2021059870

ISBN: 9781032034508 (hbk)
ISBN: 9781032034485 (pbk)
ISBN: 9781003187349 (ebk)

DOI: 10.4324/9781003187349

Typeset in Sabon
by Newgen Publishing UK

Contents

Preface

Through researching and writing about workplace bullying and harassment over the past decade, I have learned that workplace bullying and harassment are a big thing, and also part of a bigger thing known as psychosocial hazards (PSH)—work factors that have the potential to lead to physical or psychological injury and work-related stress if not managed correctly.

Realization of the increasingly significant role of PSHs in the work environment, and of the lack of awareness of them by U.S. agencies and organizations, in large part prompted this book. Its aim is to impress upon U.S. employers the need to ensure workers' psychological health and safety in the world of work by introducing the measures for doing so that are being implemented in numerous countries and globally pursuant to legislation, guidance, and a global standard. Measures implemented in Europe, individual European countries, Canada, Mexico, Australia, and Japan, as well as discussion of the global standard ISO45003, attempt to capture the progress being made globally and to offer models for U.S. employers.

Emphasis is placed on the imperative for occupational health and safety, human resources, and management to work together rather than in silos, as well as to expand traditional thinking about roles in and views of the work environment. While this may seem an unfamiliar concept to U.S. employers, treating workers' psychological health and safety as equivalent to their physical health and safety demands inclusion in the evolving workplace.

This book began taking shape well before the global COVID-19 pandemic. However, COVID-19 and its accompanying challenges for the world of work have accelerated the need for U.S. agencies and organizations to move psychological health and safety to the forefront of workplace concerns, sharing equal space with physical health and safety.

Finally, while it is far from simple to address the wide scope of PSHs that can lead to physical or psychological injuries in the modern world of work – indeed, it is both complex and multidimensional—that is exactly where we need to get to in the United States, now more than ever. My hope for this book is that it will contribute to moving us forward in meeting this challenge. The U.S. workplace has much to gain from doing so.

Part I

Work-related Stress, Psychosocial Hazards, and the U.S. Workplace

Part I provides global definitions of work-related stress and psychosocial hazards (PSH) and risks, defined as those aspects of the design and management of work, and its social and organizational context, that have the potential to cause psychological and physical harm if not managed correctly. It is anticipated that psychosocial risks will be more pervasive than traditional occupational safety and health hazards in future work environments. The United States lags behind much of the world in addressing PSH at work, although progress is being made by the National Institute for Occupational Safety and Health and its Total Worker Health program.

DOI: 10.4324/9781003187349-1

Chapter 1

Today's World of Work

Work-related Stress and Psychosocial Hazards

Terminology and Global Definitions of Work-related Stress and Psychosocial Hazards

Exposure to psychosocial hazards, if not managed well, may result in stress to the worker.

Today's world of work is more complex than ever before. The consequences of the change from an industrial to a service economy, as well as green and demographic transitions, have increased the psychosocial hazards (PSH) and work-related stress that exist in the modern world of work. COVID-19 has presented a further challenge to the workplace.

Rates of work-related stress and burnout are high, and continue to rise in the United States and globally, often caused by psychosocial hazards—workplace factors that can cause stress.

Work-related stress, an occupational hazard, is an omnipresent term for a very good reason: work is the number 1 source of stress in the United States:

- The American Institute of Stress states that job stress costs U.S. employers more than $300 billion annually (Pfeffer, 2018, p. 2).
- According to a Gallup study, daily employee stress worldwide reached a record high 43 percent in 2020.

Taking care of psychological health and safety at work is about protecting the psychological health of workers, just as we protect their physical health. Exposure to psychosocial risks is becoming increasingly common and, if not managed well, may result in stress to the worker. Decreases in physical risks at work are occurring due to the decline of industrial society, while there are increases in psychological risk with rise of service industries (Montgomery et al., 2020, p. 123).

DOI: 10.4324/9781003187349-2

Terminology

An increasing recognition of the importance of employees' psychological health and the necessity of organizations managing psychosocial hazards and work-related stress has brought numerous terms into the vocabulary.

> One of the biggest impediments to progress on work-related psychological harm is the inexactitude of the terminology used.
>
> (Jones, 2020)

For this reason, it is helpful to offer a sampling of global terms and definitions.

Work-related Stress

> Work-related stress is the physical, mental and emotional reactions that occur when a worker perceives the demands of their work exceed their ability or resources to cope. Work-related stress if prolonged and/or severe can cause both psychological and physical harm. The longer that the work-related stresses continue unresolved, the higher the risk that a psychological injury will occur.
>
> (SafeWorkSA 2020. Mental Health)

> Stress is not an injury or an illness, however excessive and long-lasting stress can have a negative effect on employees' health, safety and wellbeing and can lead to psychological injury. Work-related stress is recognised globally as a major occupational health and safety (OHS) hazard and can be challenging for employers to prevent and manage. Guidance … can help employers recognise psychosocial hazards that, if left unmanaged, may increase the risk of stress and psychological injury.
>
> (WorkSafe Victoria 2021)

> [Stress is] the harmful physical and emotional response caused by an imbalance between the perceived demands and the perceived resources and abilities of individuals to cope with those demands. Work-related stress is determined by work organization, work design and labour relations and occurs when the demands of the job do not match or exceed the capabilities, resources, or needs of the worker, or when the knowledge or abilities of an individual worker or group to cope are not matched with the expectations of the organizational culture of an enterprise.
>
> (International Labour Organization, 2016, pp 2–4)

[Work-related stress] emerges when the knowledge and abilities to cope of an individual worker or of a group are not matched with the demands of the job and expectations of the organizational culture of an enterprise. It becomes a risk to health and safety when work exceeding the worker's capacity, resources and ability to cope is prolonged.

(International Labour Organization, 2015)

Worker stress is a physiological and/or psychological reaction to an event that is perceived to be threatening or taxing. Work stressor is an interaction between a worker and some environmental event with a physical or psychological reaction in nature or both.

(Reggio, 2003, pp. 247–48)

EU-OSHA has adopted the following definition: Work-related stress is experienced when the demands of the work environment exceed the workers' ability to cope with (or control) them.

(EU-OSHA, 2002)

[Stress is] a state, which is accompanied by physical, psychological or social complaints or dysfunctions and which results from individuals feeling unable to bridge a gap with the requirements or expectations placed on them.

(EU Framework Agreement on Work-Related Stress, 2004)

Stress is commonly defined as a perceived imbalance between the demands made on people and their resources or ability to cope with those demands. Although the experience of stress might appear primarily psychological, stress also affects physical health. The symptoms of stress can result in increased absenteeism, high turnover, disciplinary problems, violence and psychological harassment, reduced productivity, as well as reduced attention, mistakes and accidents.

Factors, both inside and outside the workplace, can influence health. Poorly managed work features, such as constant high job demands, tight deadlines, harassment, and unsupportive managerial style, are likely to provoke the feeling of stress in workers. Legally, all employers have a general duty to ensure the health and safety of workers in every aspect of their work

(Mexicolaws.com, 2019)

Psychosocial hazards at work are not equivalent to stress at work; rather, if they are not prevented, they may lead to stress and stress-related outcomes.

> Psychosocial refers to a combination of psychological and social factors.
>
> (Lerouge, 2017, pp. 385–386)

> Psychosocial hazards and factors are anything in the design or management of work that increases the risk of psychological harm. The hazards may be related to job demands (workplace factors that can cause stress) and job resources (workplace factors that can protect a worker from stress) that have been identified in research.
>
> (Jain et al., 2017, p. 3632)

The concept of psychosocial factors refers to interactions between work, the environment, job satisfaction and organizational conditions, as well as the worker's capabilities, needs, culture, and their personal situation outside of work considering their experiences and perceptions.

Psychosocial hazards relate to how work is organized, social factors at work, aspects of the work environment, equipment, and hazardous tasks. In other words, work-related stress is determined by psychosocial hazards found in work organization, work design, working conditions, and labor relations.

When reference is made to psychosocial hazards, it is implied that these aspects of work organization, design and management have the potential to cause harm to individual health and safety as well as leading to other adverse organizational outcomes (Jain et al., 2021, p. 3632).

Psychosocial hazards can be present in all organizations and sectors, and can result from all kinds of work tasks, equipment, and employment arrangements. They often interact with one another and with other types of hazards in the work environment. When psychosocial hazards are not managed effectively, they can increase risks to psychological health, physical health, and organizational outcomes.

Definitions of Psychosocial Factors, Psychosocial Hazards, and Psychosocial Risks

A psychosocial factor is a neutral term, not carrying a negative or positive connotation, but a psychosocial hazard is not.

Psychosocial factors are elements within the influence and responsibility of employers that can impact the psychological health and safety of employees, both positively and negatively. How and when work is assigned, deadlines, workload, work methods, work relationships, and interactions are all part of psychosocial factors (Guarding Minds @Work, 2021).

A hazard is a situation or thing that has the potential to harm a person. Hazards include elements of the work environment, management practices, and/or organizational dimensions that increase the risk to health.

Psychosocial hazards result from deficiencies in the design, organization, and management of work. A psychosocial hazard may be anything in the design or management of work and its social and organizational contexts, such as the ways people interact with each other, which can cause stress and has the potential for causing psychological and physical harm.

Psychosocial hazards can lead to work-related stress and organizational stressors:

> While hazard refers to the intrinsic property or potential capacity of an agent, process or situation (including work organization and working practices) to cause harm or adverse health at work, the term risk describes the combination of the likelihood of a hazardous event and the severity of health damage to a worker caused by this event. Thus, psychosocial risk refers to the likelihood or probability that a person will be harmed or experience adverse health effects if exposed to a psychosocial hazard.
>
> (International Labour Organization, 2016)

> Psychosocial hazards can lead to psychological injury and/or physical harm. Psychosocial hazards are work factors that have the potential to cause psychological and/or physical harm. These arise from the design and/or management of work and/or the way people interact with each other. When psychosocial hazards are not effectively managed, they increase risks to psychological health.
>
> (NSW Government, 2021)

Psychosocial risks occur due to exposure to psychosocial hazards. Psychosocial risk is defined as the potential of psychosocial hazards to cause harm:

> Psychosocial risks may arise from poor work design, organization, and management, as well as a poor social context of work, and they may result in negative psychological, physical, and social outcomes such as work-related stress, burnout or depression. Some examples of working conditions leading to psychosocial risks include psychological and sexual harassment.
>
> (European Agency for Safety and Health at Work, 2021)

Belgian law defines psychosocial risks (PSR) as:

> the likelihood that one or more workers will suffer psychological damage, which may or not be combined with physical damage, as a result of exposure to a work situation which entails a risk. This hazardous work situation may relate to the organization of the work,

the employment conditions, occupational health and safety, the content of the work or interpersonal relationships at work.

(FPS Employment, Labour and Social Dialogue, 2016, p. 9)

Global Standard ISO45003 (2021) defines psychosocial risk as

a combination of the likelihood of occurrence of exposure to work-related hazard(s) of a psychosocial nature and the severity of injury and ill-health that can be caused by these hazards. Hazards of a psychosocial nature include aspects of work organization, social factors at work, work environment, equipment, and hazardous tasks.

(ISO 2021, pp. 11–13)

Mexico's Nom-035 states Psychosocial Risk Factors "are those that can cause anxiety disorders, a non-organic sleep-wake cycle and severe stress and adaptation derived from the nature of the functions of the job position in the workplace, the type of work shift and the exposure to severe traumatic events or acts of labor violence to the worker, for the work carried out.

(Mexlaws.com, 2018)

The U.K. Health and Safety Executive states that psychosocial risk factors are things that may affect workers' psychological response to their work and workplace conditions (including working relationships with supervisors and colleagues). Psychosocial risk management is thus the management of risks associated with the work organization and the social context of work, which have the potential to cause psychological and physical ill-health.

Fluid Terminology

The definition of stress and the terminology used to refer to psychosocial hazards and risks has changed over the years, from stressors or stress factors to psychosocial factors, psychosocial hazards, or psychosocial risks.

The terms "psychosocial hazards" and "psychosocial risks" are sometimes used interchangeably in the literature. Although there is a reasonable consensus in the scientific community regarding the nature of psychosocial hazards, "it should be noted that new forms of work and the changing working environment give rise to new hazards; and therefore the definition of psychosocial hazards can still evolve." (International Labour Organization, 2016, pp. 2–4). Psychological health means mental health, and a range of terms are used in relation as to the effect of psychosocial hazards and risks, including "mental health" and "psychological health." Generally, these terms can be used interchangeably.

Regardless of how they are defined, exposure to psychosocial hazards and risks are becoming increasingly common:

> Psychosocial risks have now been acknowledged as global issues, affecting all countries, profession and workers.
>
> (Lerouge, 2017, p. v)

> Employers must understand what constitutes health risks in the work environments, and that includes the psychosocial risks that are today more omnipotent than the risks of physical injury.
>
> (Pfeffer, 2018, p. 3)

> Psychosocial hazards can occur in combination with one another and can influence and be influenced by other hazards.
>
> (International Standards Organization, 2021, p. 3)

Employees are likely to be exposed to a combination of psychosocial hazards. Some might always be present at work, while others are present only occasionally. There is a greater risk of work-related stress when psychosocial hazards combine and act together, so employers should never consider hazards in isolation.

Relationship Between Psychosocial and Physical Hazards

There is growing recognition that poor psychological work health and safety can lead to both psychological and physical injuries. Moreover, psychosocial risks can manifest in physical as well as mental ill-health:

> Work-related physical hazards and psychosocial hazards can be connected, and one can affect the other. Employees who do not feel safe at work due to physical hazards can be at risk of developing work-related stress. Employees who are stressed have a higher risk of musculoskeletal disorders (MSDs) and their concentration and decision-making abilities can be affected, increasing the risk of physical injury.
>
> (WorkSafe Victoria, 2021)

> Studies have found that "psychosocial" factors, such as work-related stress, are the most important variables in determining the length of a life.
>
> (Lehrer, 2011)

Stress at Work: Objective or Subjective?

Although job design and workplace environment impact a worker's mental health and the way they respond to stressors, not all workers respond to stress in the same manner or to the same extent. How is this situation taken into account in determining what working conditions are stressful?

> Despite work-related stress being such a widespread issue with many associated negative health effects, stress is also a very personal experience. Workers exposed to the same source or kind of stress will not necessarily respond in the same way, because of subtle individual and environmental differences.
>
> (Cunningham, 2020)

Belgium provides guidance on objective danger. To speak of psychosocial risks at work, it must be a question of situations that contain a danger from an objective point of view: the subjective experience of the individual worker is not decisive:

> The danger is objective when it could cause damage to mental health (possibly accompanied by physical damage) to any average worker placed in the same circumstances. If the situation can be considered normal, the employer cannot be held responsible for the suffering of the worker.
>
> (FPS Employment, Labor and Social Dialogue, 2021)

However, consequences differ depending on the factors specific to the individual:

> The fact that some workers are more vulnerable because of events connected with their personal lives does not relieve the company of its responsibility and its obligation to prevent occupational risks.
>
> (FPS Employment, Labour and Social Dialogue, 2016, p. 14)

The World Health Organization makes the following points about stress as it impacts individual workers:

> Although individual and organizational characteristics play a role in the development of work-related stress, the majority will agree that work-related stress results from the interaction between the worker and the conditions of work. Views differ, however, on the importance of worker characteristics versus working conditions as the primary cause of stress. These differences are important, since they suggest and lead to different ways to prevent the source of stress at work.

One view promotes that individual differences of the worker, such as personality, age, education, experience and coping style are most important in predicting whether certain job specifications will result in stress. These individual differences demand complementary prevention strategies that focus on the individual and promote ways of coping with demanding working conditions.

However, the prevailing view based on evidence is that certain working conditions are stressful to most people. Stressful working conditions are related to psychosocial hazards, such as too high or too low job demands, a fast work pace or time pressure, a lack of control over work load and work processes, lack of social support from colleagues and/or supervisors, discrimination, isolation, psychological harassment, lack of participation in decision making, poor communication or information flow, job insecurity, lack of opportunity for growth, lack of advancement or promotion, irregular working hours (especially shift work), and being exposed to unpleasant or dangerous physical conditions, and not being able to control them. Here, prevention strategies focus on changing working conditions or job redesign.
(Houtman & Jettinghof, 2007, p. 17)

Regardless of the type of measurement applied, consequences from stressful working conditions for organizations and employees may be significant now more than ever.

References and Further Reading

Chirico, F. (2017). The forgotten realm of the new and emerging psychosocial risk factors. *Journal of Occupational Health*, 59(5), 433–435.

Cunningham, C. J. L. (2020). Psychological and social determinants of health, safety, and well-being at work: The occupational health psychology perspective. Available at www.aiha.org/blog/psychological-and-social-determinants-of-health-safety-and-well-being-at-work-the-occupational-health-psychology-perspective. Accessed September 24, 2021.

EU Framework Agreement on Work-Related Stress. (2004). Website. Available at https://osha.europa.eu/en/legislation/guidelines/framework-agreement-work-related-stress. Accessed November 2, 2021.

EU-OSHA. (2002). Factsheet 22: Work-related stress. Available at https://osha.europa.eu/en/publications/factsheets/22. Accessed October 28, 2021.

European Agency for Safety and Health at Work. (2021). Psychosocial risks and stress at work. Available at https://osha.europa.eu/en/themes/psychosocial-risks-and-stress. Accessed October 12, 2021.

FPS Employment, Labor and Social Dialogue. (2021). Psychosocial risks at work: Definition and scope. Available at https://emploi.belgique.be/fr/themes/bien-etre-au-travail/risques-psychosociaux-au-travail/definitions-et-champ-dapplication. Accessed September 18, 2021.

FPS Employment, Labour and Social Dialogue. (2016). Guide to the prevention of psychosocial risks at work. Available at https://employment.belgium.be/sites/default/files/content/publications/PSR_Guide_prevention_EN_2020.pdf. Accessed July 19, 2021.

Guarding Minds@Work. (2021). Know the psychosocial factors. Available at www.guardingmindsatwork.ca/about/about-psychosocial-factors. Accessed July 29, 2021.

Houtman, I. & Jettinghoff, K. (2007). *Raising awareness of stress at work in developing countries A modern hazard in a traditional working environment.* Geneva: World Health Organization. Available at www.who.int/occupational _health/publications/raisingawarenessofstress.pdf. Accessed October 8, 2021.

International Labour Organization. (2015). Psychosocial risks and work-related stress. Available at www.ilo.org/global/topics/safety-and-health-at-work/area sofwork/workplace-health-promotion-and-well-being/WCMS_108557/lang--en/index.htm. Accessed October 28, 2021.

International Labour Organization. (2016). Workplace stress: A collective challenge. Available at www.ilo.org/safework/info/publications/WCMS_466 547/lang--en/index.htm. Accessed July 19, 2021.

International Standards Organization (ISO). (2021). ISO 45003. Available at www.iso.org/obp/ui/#iso:std:iso:45003:ed-1:v1:en. Accessed October 28, 2021.

Jain, A., Hassard, J., Leka, S., Di Tecco, C., & Iavicoli, S. (2017). The role of occupational health services in psychosocial risk management and the promotion of mental health and well-being at work. *International Journal of Environmental Research and Public Health*, 18(7), 3632.

Jones, K. (2020, December 24). Right information, wrong magazine. *SafetyAtWorkBlog.* Available at https://safetyatworkblog.com/2020/12/24.

Lehrer, J. (2011, August 20). Your co-workers might be killing you. *Wall Street Journal.* Available at www.wsj.com/articles/SB100014240531119033929 04576512233116576352. Accessed October 26, 2021.

Leka, S. & Jain, A. (2010). Health impact of psychosocial hazards at work: An overview. Nottingham: Institute of Work, Health & Organisations, University of Nottingham. Available at https://apps.who.int/iris/bitstream/handle/10665/44428/?sequence=1. Accessed October 29, 2021

Lerouge, L. (Ed.) (2017). *Psychosocial risks in labour and social security law.* New York: Springer.

Mexlaws.com (2018). M-035-STPS-2018: Occupational psychosocial risk factors—Identification, analysis and prevention. Available at www.mexl aws.com/STPS/NOM-035-STPS-2018-information.htm. Accessed October 12, 2021.

Montgomery, A., van der Doef, M., Panagopoulou, E., & Leiter, M. P. (Eds.). (2020). *Connecting healthcare worker well-being, patient safety and organisational change. Work-related psychosocial risks: key definitions and an overview of the policy context in Europe.* New York: Springer.

NSW Government. (2021). *Code of practice: Managing psychosocial hazards at work.* Sydney: Safework NSW. Available at www.safework.nsw.gov.au/__data/assets/pdf_file/0004/983353/Code-of-Practice_Managing-psychosocial-haza rds.pdf. Accessed November 10, 2021.

Pfeffer, J. (2018). *Dying for a paycheck: How modern management harms employee health and company performance—and what we can do about it.* New York: HarperBusiness.

Reggio, R. E. (2003). *Introduction to industrial/organizational psychology,* 4th edn. Englewood Cliffs, NJ: Prentice-Hall.

SafeWork Australia. (2020). *Psychosocial health and safety and bullying in Australian workplaces: Summary of findings.* Available at www.safeworkau stralia.gov.au/resources-and-publications/statistical-reports/psychosocial-hea lth-and-safety-and-bullying-australian-workplaces-3rd-edition-summary-findi ngs. Accessed November 15, 2021.

SafeWork Australia. (2021). Infographic: Managing psychosocial hazards at work. Available at www.safeworkaustralia.gov.au/doc/infographic-managing-psychosocial-hazards-work. Accessed November 8, 2021.

SafeWork SA. (2020). Psychological hazards & work-related stress. Available at www.safework.sa.gov.au/workers/health-and-wellbeing/psychological-haza rds. Accessed November 8, 2021.

WorkSafe Victoria. (2021). Preventing and managing work-related stress: A guide for employers. Available at www.worksafe.vic.gov.au/preventing-and-managing-work-related-stress-guide-employers. Accessed July 19, 2021.

Chapter 2

Psychosocial Hazard Specifics

Psychosocial Hazards and Risks: An International Compilation

Psychosocial risks are not always easy to identify. Their sources are many and varied, and the risks occur at every level of the organization:

> Stressful psychosocial factors in the working environment include physical aspects, some aspects of the organisation and system of work, and the quality of human relations in the enterprise. All these factors interact and affect the psychological climate in the enterprise and the physical and mental health of workers.
>
> (International Labour Organization, 1986, pp. 1–3)

Chapter 1 discussed how psychosocial hazards (PSH) relate to the way work is organized, social factors at work, and aspects of the work environment. Psychosocial risks arise from poor work design, organization, and management, as well as a poor social context of work.

The detailed breakdown offered in this Chapter provides more in-depth specifics:

- *Organization of work:* the way tasks are structured and distributed within a company, as well as the relationships of authority designed to achieve the company's objectives.
- *Content of work:* factors such as the complexity of the tasks, the intellectual or manual nature of the work, and the required skills. In terms of workload, some refer specifically to the emotional strain (contact with the public, encountering suffering, having to hide one's emotions).
- *Relationships at work:* Labor relations, or interpersonal relationships at work, are the social relationships between workers and the social relationships between the worker and the organization that employs them. Relationships with third parties, customers, and suppliers are also included.

DOI: 10.4324/9781003187349-3

- *Employment conditions:*
  - Type of work pattern: flexible working hours, shift work, night work, part-time work, overtime, split shifts;
  - *Type of contract:* short-term contracts, consecutive contracts, part-time contracts;
  - Wage and social benefits;
  - The ways in which the work is assessed;
  - Training and career opportunities;
  - Options for planning working hours;
  - Work–life balance. (Federal Public Service Employment, Labour and Social Dialogue, 2016)

International Compilation of PSH

Based on a review of country and global laws, guidance, and standards, hazards of a psychosocial nature may arise out of the following:

- Organizational and workgroup culture;
- Aspects of how work is organized;
- Excessive workload;
- Excessive demands or conflicts in the working environment;
- Bullying, harassment, and violence at work;
- Psychological and sexual harassment;
- Violence from third parties—verbal or physical, or threat of violence;
- Poor management of change – not being involved and informed in organizational changes;
- Lack of civility and respect;
- Lack of recognition and reward;
- Interpersonal relationships and conflicts, negative leadership and supervision;
- Poor management of organizational changes;
- Social support—lack of support from management or colleagues;
- Lack of control over work and working methods/workload management;
- Lack of influence in the way in which work is carried out;
- Lack of participation in decision-making that affect the worker;
- Lack of personal control—having an inadequate say over how work is done;
- Inadequate support from managers or co-workers;
- Environmental working conditions;
- Lack of role clarity—contradictory demands and lack of clarity of the functions of the position;
- Ineffective communication;
- Job insecurity;
- Work–life balance (also known as work–life interface).

Psychosocial hazards may also be related to new forms of employment contracts, the aging workforce, work intensification, digital surveillance, and poor work–life balance (Schulte, 2020).

Psychosocial hazards may interact, such as in a case where an employee has high demands and little control over how they meet those demands; this employee is more likely to experience stress.

Categories of Hazards of a Psychosocial Nature

ISO 45003, Psychological Health and Safety at Work—Guidelines for Managing Psychosocial Risks (International Standardization Organization, 2021) is the first global standard created to help organizations identify and control psychosocial hazards. It categorizes hazards of a psychosocial nature into how work is organized; social factors at work; and work environment, work equipment, and hazardous tasks. A comprehensive list of examples is included under these categories.

How work is organized includes roles and expectations, job control or autonomy, job demands, organizational change management, remote and isolated work, workload and work pace, working hours and schedule, and job security and precarious work. Specific examples cited include:

- Role ambiguity;
- Role conflict;
- Lack of clear guidelines on expected tasks;
- Uncertainty about or frequent changes to tasks and work standards;
- Job demands, workload, and work pace;
- Performing work of little value or purpose;
- Limited opportunities to participate in decision-making; lack of control over workload;
- Low levels of influence and independence;
- Conflicting demands and deadlines;
- Unrealistic expectations of a worker's competence or responsibilities;
- Lack of task variety or performing highly repetitive tasks;
- Exposure to events or situations that can cause trauma;
- Lack of practical support provided to assist workers during transition periods;
- Working alone in non-remote locations without social/human interaction at work;
- Work overload or underload;
- High levels of time pressure;
- High levels of repetitive work;
- Lack of variety of work;
- Shiftwork;

- Inflexible work schedules;
- Unpredictable hours;
- Uncertainty regarding work availability;
- Long hours;
- The possibility of redundancy or temporary loss of work with reduced pay.

Social factors at work include interpersonal relationships, leadership, organizational/workgroup culture, recognition and reward, career development, support, supervision, civility and respect, work–life balance, violence at work, harassment, bullying, and victimization. Specific examples cited include:

- Poor relationships between managers, supervisors, co-workers, and clients or others with whom workers interact;
- Interpersonal conflict;
- Harassment, bullying, victimization (including using electronic tools such as email and social media);
- Lack of social support;
- Unequal power relationships between dominant and non-dominant groups of workers;
- Social or physical isolation;
- Lack of clear vision and objectives;
- Management style unsuited to the nature of the work and its demands;
- Failing to listen or only casually listening to complaints and suggestions;
- Withholding information;
- Providing inadequate communication and support;
- Lack of accountability;
- Lack of fairness in decision-making;
- Inconsistent and poor decision-making practices;
- Abuse or misuse of power;
- Low levels of support for problem-solving and personal development;
- Inconsistent and untimely application of policies and procedures;
- Imbalance between workers' effort recognition and reward;
- Lack of appropriate acknowledgment and appreciation of workers' efforts in a fair and timely manner;
- Work tasks, roles, schedules, or expectations causing workers to continue working in their own time;
- Conflicting demands of work and home;
- Work that impacts the workers' ability to recover;
- Incidents involving an explicit or implicit challenge to health, safety or wellbeing at work;

- Offensive, intimidating behaviors (sexual or non-sexual) relating to one or more specific characteristics of the targeted individual; and
- Repeated unreasonable behaviors which can present a risk to health, safety and wellbeing at work.

Specific examples of *work environment, work equipment, and hazardous tasks* include:

- Inadequate equipment availability, suitability, reliability, maintenance or repair;
- Poor workplace conditions such as lack of space, poor lighting and excessive noise;
- Lack of the necessary tools, equipment, or other resources to complete work tasks;
- Working in extreme conditions or situations, such as very high or low temperatures, or at height.

Violence, Bullying, and Sexual Harassment

Psychosocial hazards include aggressive or abusive behaviors, including bullying and violence at the workplace—these are the most extreme forms of psychosocial risks at work.

It is impossible to discuss psychosocial hazards without specifically mentioning bullying, perhaps the most legally recognized PSH. Bullying is a PSH and a stress that may arise from interactions with other employees, such as supervisors or co-workers. ISO 45003 defines bullying as

> repeated (more than once) unreasonable behaviors which can present a risk to health, safety and wellbeing at work. Behaviors can be overt or covert, e.g., social or physical isolation; assigning meaningless or unfavorable work tasks; name calling, insults and intimidation; undermining behavior; undue public criticism; withholding resources critical for one's job/malicious rumors or gossiping; assigning impossible deadlines.
>
> (International Standardization Organization,
> 2021. ISO 45003)

Bullying and harassment have increasingly been recognized among the working conditions leading to psychosocial risks. In recent years, issues such as harassment, violence, and bullying at work have more explicitly been recognized as psychosocial hazards.

Psychosocial risks and their consequences, such as stress, as well as violence and harassment at work, are all closely interrelated, and often act as contributing causes for and consequences of one another, affecting the wellbeing and occupational health and safety of workers:

> The interrelationship between work-related stress and violence develops when violence and harassment generate elevated stress levels affecting both the victims and witnesses among the co-workers. Furthermore, violence and harassment may occur as a result of work-related stress and psychosocial hazards. Conflicts arising from poor work organization that were not properly managed can also be a source of violence. Workplace organization and design, together with work intensity, are other relevant factors, as workers experiencing stress, conflict and/or isolation are at risk of psychosocial harm.
>
> (International Labour Organization, 2016)

Sexual Harassment as a Psychosocial Hazard

The #MeToo movement, which started in the United States, sparked a worldwide conversation about sexual harassment, leading to increased attention and legislation. Sexual harassment is treated as a psychosocial hazard in numerous definitions and laws globally. In the context of this book, sexual harassment is referred to primarily as a PSH, but is not discussed specifically as a separate topic. (For more information on sexual harassment laws and developments around the world, see Cobb, 2020.)

The psychosocial hazards of workplace bullying and sexual harassment often arise due to a power imbalance, specifically an abuse of power between a supervisor and subordinate.

What are Not Psychosocial Hazards?

It is essential not to confuse the demands of the job, with hazardous psychosocial factors such as an excessive workload and risks, with situations that, while stimulating and sometimes challenging, offer a work environment in which the worker is supported, receives the appropriate training and is motivated to perform their job in the best possible way (EU-OSHA, 2021).[1]

On the Flip Side: Traits of a Positive Psychosocial Environment

> A psychologically healthy and safe workplace is a workplace that promotes workers' psychological wellbeing and actively works to prevent harm to worker psychological health including in negligent, reckless, or intentional ways.
>
> (Guarding Minds@Work, 2021)

Mexican law Nom-035 refers to a favorable organizational environment as one in which the employer must carry out actions that promote the sense of belonging of the workers to the organization.

Traits of a positive psychosocial environment include:

- *Organizational culture:* good psychosocial safety climate; clear organizational mission and objectives; good communication; available support for problems; good physical working conditions;
- *Employee role in the organization:* strong communication regarding employee's role and responsibilities in organization; support to meet objectives; encouragement and recognition from employer;
- *Job content and control:* meaningful work; consultation for job-related decision making; appropriate use of the worker's skills and experience; employee engagement;
- *Workload and schedule:* appropriate workload and reasonable working hours; reasonable work pace and deadlines; flexible options for work;
- *Interpersonal work relationships:* appropriate policies and procedures regarding workplace conduct, respect in the workplace, and diversity, equity, and inclusion, social support and teamwork, employee recognition and reward;
- *Acknowledgement of work–life balance:* Right to disconnect electronically after work hours.

See Chapter 22 for more traits of a positive psychosocial environment.

Attention to psychosocial hazards in the workplace is not new. As far back as 1984, the International Labour Organization (ILO)[2] defined psychosocial factors (hazards) in terms of "interactions between and among work environment, job content, organizational conditions and workers' capacities, needs, culture, personal extra-job considerations that may, through perceptions and experience, influence health, work performance and job satisfaction" (International Labour Organization, 1984, pp. 2–4)

The ILO, in conjunction with the World Health Organization (International Labour Organization, 1984), referred to psychosocial risk factors as those conditions present in a work situation, related to the organization, the content and the performance of the task, likely to affect both the wellbeing and physical, mental or social health of the workers as well as the development of the work, causing stress and even burnout.

The International Labor Organization and World Health Organization meeting included the agenda item "Identification and Control of Adverse Psychosocial Factors at Work," and noted that adverse occupational psychosocial factors have become increasingly significant (International Labour Organization, 1984).

Notes

1 For a review that systematically investigates working conditions in the gig economy and their potential for causing psychosocial harm, see Bérastégui (2021).
2 The International Labour Organization is a tripartite United Nations agency that brings together governments, employers, and workers of 187 member states, sets labor standards, develops policies and devises programs promoting decent work for all.

References and Further Reading

Bérastégui, P. (2021). *Exposure to psychosocial risk factors in the gig economy: A systematic review by ETUI.* Available at www.etui.org/sites/default/files/2021-01/Exposure%20to%20psychosocial%20risk%20factors%20in%20the%20gig%20economy-a%20systematic%20review-web-2021.pdf. Accessed June 2, 2021.

Cobb, E. P. (2020) *International sexual harassment laws for the multinational employer.* London: Routledge.

EU-OSHA. (2014). *E-guide to managing stress and psychosocial risks.* Available at https://osha.europa.eu/en/tools-and-resources/e-guides/e-guide-managing-stress-and-psychosocial-risks. Accessed July 19, 2021.

EU-OSHA. (2021). Psychosocial risks and stress at work. Available at https://osha.europa.eu/en/themes/psychosocial-risks-and-stress. Accessed November 3, 2021.

Federal Public Service Employment, Labour and Social Dialogue. (2016). *Guide to the prevention of psychosocial risks at work.* Available at https://employment.belgium.be/sites/default/files/content/publications/PSR_Guide_prevention_EN_2020.pdf. Accessed October 29, 2021.

Guarding Minds@Work. (2021). Website. Available at https://guardingmindsatwork.ca. Accessed November 17, 2021.

International Labour Organization. (1984). *Psychosocial factors at work: Recognition and control. Report of the Joint ILO/WHO Committee on Occupational Health Ninth Session Geneva, 18–24 September 1984.* Available at www.who.int/occupational_health/publications/ILO_WHO_1984_report_of_the_joint_committee.pdf. Accessed September 27, 2021.

International Labour Organization. (2016). Special issue: Psychosocial risks, stress and violence in the world of work. *International Journal of Labour Research,* 8(1–2). Available at www.ilo.org/wcmsp5/groups/public/---ed_dialogue/---actrav/documents/publication/wcms_551796.pdf. Accessed October 21, 2021.

International Labour Organization. (2016). *Workplace stress: A collective challenge.* Available at www.ilo.org/wcmsp5/groups/public/---ed_protect/---protrav/---safework/documents/publication/wcms_466547.pdf. Accessed July 19, 2021.

International Standardization Organization. (2021). *ISO 45003.* Available at www.iso.org/obp/ui/#iso:std:iso:45003:ed-1:v1:en. Accessed October 28, 2021.

Mexlaws.com. (2018). *NOM-035-STPS-2018: Occupational psychosocial risk factors – Identification, analysis and prevention*. Available at www.mexl aws.com/STPS/NOM-035-STPS-2018-information.htm. Accessed October 12, 2021.

Schulte, P. A. (2020). A global perspective on addressing occupational safety and health hazards in the future of work. *La Medicina del Lavoro*, 111(3), 163–165.

Wynne, R., De Broeck, V., Vandenbroek, K., Leka, S., Jain, A., Houtman, I., & McDaid, D. (2014). *Promoting mental health in the workplace: Guidance to implementing a comprehensive approach*. The Hague: European Commission. Available at www.researchgate.net/publication/277476748_Promoting_ mental_health_in_the_workplace_guidance_to_implementing_a_comprehensi ve_approach. Accessed November 14, 2021.

Chapter 3

Why the Psychosocial Environment Matters

Effects on Employees

The work environment and work organization can significantly impact the mental health and wellbeing of workers. Good working conditions can benefit good mental health and negative working conditions, or occupational risks, can contribute to or exacerbate existing mental or physical health problems.

The psychosocial work environment relates to psychosocial factors at work, which are aspects of work organization, design, and management that include work demands, the availability of organizational support, rewards and interpersonal relationships in the workplace. Whether an organization has a positive or negative psychosocial work environment will depend on how effectively it manages psychosocial risk associated with its various dimensions: "The work environment affects how people think about their lives and also their level of psychological wellbeing" (Pfeffer, 2018, p. 30). Research has established the effects of workplace environments on health, "and yet the management literature, organizational leaders, and public policy practitioners pay astonishingly little attention to the role of workplace environments" (Pfeffer, 2018, pp. 192–193).

Health Problems

If not adequately controlled, psychosocial hazards can lead to psychological and physical health problems, including work-related anxiety, depression, alcohol and drug abuse, post-traumatic stress, suicide, musculoskeletal disorders, and other physical illnesses. They can also increase the likelihood of developing a mental disorder, or of an existing mental disorder becoming worse, as well as negatively impacting the safety and the health of the organization.

DOI: 10.4324/9781003187349-4

Effects on employees include:

- Work-related stress;
- Anxiety and depression;
- Low mood;
- Low motivation;
- Burnout;
- Sleeplessness;
- Exhaustion;
- Musculoskeletal disorders;
- Physical illnesses, such as stomach aches, headaches, and increased blood pressure;
- Muscular tension and ergonomic issues;
- Cognitive impairment;
- Eating or substance abuse disorders; and
- Suicidal thoughts, suicide attempts, and completed suicide.

A range of physical reactions can also occur, such as digestive problems, changes to appetite and weight, dermatological reactions, fatigue, cardiovascular disease, musculoskeletal disorders, headaches or other unexplained aches and pains. There may be changes in behaviors, such as altered activity levels or increased use of tobacco, alcohol, and drugs as a way of coping, in addition to changes in the person's ability to relax or their level of irritability (International Labour Organization, 2020).

A Fine Balance

The International Labour Organization's observation on work environments and mental health offers a cautionary note:

> Changing working environments undoubtedly bring opportunities, for professional development, expanding networks and innovation. The extent and pace of change can, however, when coupled with a working environment that doesn't take account of people's mental wellbeing, lead to physical and mental health problems, harmful use of alcohol or other substances, absenteeism and lost productivity. Indeed, the lost productivity resulting from depression and anxiety, two of the most common mental disorders, is estimated to cost the global economy US$1 trillion each year. Many factors influence the mental health of employees. Organizational issues include poor communication and management practices, limited participation in decision making, long or inflexible working hours and lack of team cohesion. Bullying and psychological harassment are well-known causes of work-related stress and related mental health problems.
>
> (Jones, 2020)

Full-time workers employed by organizations that fail to prioritize their employees' mental health have a threefold increased risk of being diagnosed with depression, according to a 2021 year-long population study by the University of South Australia, published in the *British Medical Journal* and led by UniSA's Psychosocial Safety Climate Observatory. Lead author Dr. Amy Zadow states that poor workplace mental health can be traced back to poor management practices, priorities, and values, which then flows through to high job demands and low resources: "Evidence shows that companies who fail to reward or acknowledge their employees for hard work, impose unreasonable demands on workers, and do not give them autonomy, are placing their staff at a much greater risk of depression" (Workplace DNA, 2021).

> An important part of controlling bullying is having a good psychosocial safety climate. Harassment and bullying at work are major contributors to stress in the workplace, and may result in very serious health problems. It is well recognized that poor psychosocial work environments facilitate harassment.
>
> (EU OSHA, 2021)

> Bullying and harassment in the workplace can have serious consequences for the physical and emotional health of workers and can also have negative effects on the organization itself, resulting in a deterioration of working conditions with significant organizational and economic consequences.
>
> (European Community Shipowners' Associations, European Transport Workers' Federation, 2013)

Effects on the Organization

Costs to the Organization of Doing Nothing

With regard to work-related stress and psychological health and safety, the financial costs to the organization of doing nothing are significant. Effects on the organization include:

- Absenteeism;
- Presenteeism and low motivation;
- Staff recruitment and retention;
- Employee commitment to work;
- Illness and injury;
- Deterioration in social climate;
- Damage to reputation;
- Legal implications;
- Customer satisfaction;

- Potential litigation;
- Disability claims.

A poor psychosocial working environment may have a considerable impact on workplace productivity, through increased absenteeism and presenteeism, lower job engagement and reduced job performance (with respect to both the quality and quantity of work). The accumulation of stress and fatigue may reduce the accuracy of work and increase the possibility of human error, heightening the risk of work injuries and accidents (International Labour Organization, 2020).

On the other hand, a work environment that promotes good psychological health and safety is socially responsible, cost-effective, helps to attract and retain good employees, and also helps an employer's bottom line.

Costs of Stress and Not Managing PSH

In discussing healthcare costs from stress-inducing work conditions, Jeffrey Pfeffer, Thomas D. Dee II Professor of Organizational Behavior at Stanford University, notes that "psychosocial elements of the work environment such as fairness, work-family conflict, high job demands, and low control over a person's work environment contribute to excess health-care costs" (Pfeffer, 2018, p. 55).

The true costs of unaddressed occupational stress are an organizational issue:

> Occupational stress may appear to be a routine and somewhat benign problem, but in reality, it contributes substantially to both economic and health-related burdens for employers. Health problems related to stress add up to employee health expenses that are almost 50 percent greater than those of unstressed employees, totaling more than $300 billion worth of losses from health costs, absenteeism and poor job performance. Such costs are incurred as employees may experience stress-induced health concerns or resort to unhealthy coping mechanisms to deal with their stress. During 2021, for example, nearly 75 percent of essential employees reported changes in weight, and 80 percent reported changes in sleep due to increased work stress. About 75 percent of these same employees in the study noted that they wanted more emotional support than they received, suggesting the correlation between unhealthy coping mechanisms and a lack of employer support.
> (Erickson, 2021)

Growing evidence indicates that unacceptable conduct is more prevalent in workplaces with poor work and organizational design, and deficient management and supervision practices:

For example, excessive time pressure, poor working environments, role conflict, perceptions of unfair application of workplace policies and procedures, where workers are regularly exposed to abuse and cultures where this is viewed as "just a normal and or an inevitable part of doing the work."

(Safework NSW, 2021)

Making employees' mental health a priority in the workplace, or ignoring it, can have significant consequences. Research shows convincingly that the psychosocial work environment impacts both the organization and its employees.

References and Further Reading

Erickson, R. A. (2021, May 7). The importance of addressing workplace stress. *Occupational Health and Stress Magazine.* Available at https://ohsonline.com/articles/2021/05/07/the-importance-of-addressing-workplace-stress.aspx?m=1. Accessed September 9, 2021.

EU-OSHA. (2021). Psychosocial risks and stress at work. Available at https://osha.europa.eu/en/news/managing-workplace-stress-by-tackling-harassment-and-bullying. Accessed November 12, 2021.

European Community Shipowners' Associations, European Transport Workers' Federation. (2013). *Eliminating workplace harassment and bullying: Guidelines to shipping companies.* Available at www.ecsa.eu/sites/default/files/2018-03/Guidelines%20to%20shipping%20companies%20EN.pdf#:~:text=We%20know%20now%20that%20bullying%20and%20harassment%20at%20the,huge%20organisational%2C%20economic%20and%20potential%20legal%20consequences%20too. Accessed November 12, 2021.

Health and Safety Executive. (2021). *Management standards for tackling work related stress.* Available at www.hse.gov.uk/stress/assets/docs/securing.pdf. Accessed November 9, 2021.

International Labour Organization. (2020). *Managing work-related psychosocial risks during the COVID-19 pandemic.* Available at www.ilo.org/wcmsp5/groups/public/---ed_protect/---protrav/---safework/documents/instructionalmaterial/wcms_748638.pdf. Accessed October 1, 2021.

Jain, A., Hassard, J., Leka, S., Di Tecco, C., & Iavicoli, S. (2017). The role of occupational health services in psychosocial risk management and the promotion of mental health and well-being at work. *International Journal of Environmental Research and Public Health*, 18(7), 3632.

Jones, K. (2020, December 24). Right information, wrong magazine. SafetyAtWorkBlog. Available at https://safetyatworkblog.com/2020/12/24. Accessed July 19, 2021.

Leka, S., Jain, A., & Lerouge, L. (2017). *Work-related psychosocial risks: Key definitions and an overview of the policy context in Europe.* Dordrecht: Springer.

Pfeffer, J. (2018). *Dying for a paycheck: How modern management harms employee health and company performance—and what we can do about it.* New York: HarperBusiness.

Safework NSW. (2021). Have your say. Available at www.haveyoursay.nsw.gov.
au/explanatory-paper-draft-code-managing-psychological-health.   Accessed
August 18, 2021.

Workplace DNA. (2021, June 30). Poor management leads to poor mental health,
report finds. Available at https://workplacedna.net/news/poor-management-
leads-poor-mental-health-report-finds. Accessed September 19, 2021.

Chapter 4

Occupational Health and Safety Basics, and Today's Evolving Framework and Scope

While risks traditionally have been viewed as physical, psychosocial health and safety, and work-related stress are increasingly entering the occupational health and safety (OHS) realm.

Traditionally, OHS has addressed the physical, chemical, and biological components of keeping workers safe but the coverage of OHS is expanding to include psychosocial hazards as the workplace changes.

Psychosocial risks and work-related stress are among the most challenging issues in occupational safety and health:

> Traditionally, the focus of Occupational Health and Safety (OHS) initiatives is on chemical, biological and physical exposures, while psychosocial risks at work are still largely neglected and their causes and consequences still insufficiently understood as they pertain to the developing country context. The current division between working conditions and the (physical) work environment makes the inclusion of the psychosocial risks at work harder to identify by most of the Occupational Health and Safety professionals.
>
> (Houtman and Jettinghoff, 2007, p. 1)

Plan, Do, Check, Act: A Brief Primer for the Non-OHS Professional

OHS Basics

In OHS, hazard identification and risk assessment are essential steps to define and adapt appropriate control measures for the workplace and the safety of its workers. (The use of OHS includes both OHS and EHS.)

DOI: 10.4324/9781003187349-5

Brief Terminology

The following are some common OHS terms.

- *Risk:* the combination of the likelihood of the occurrence of harm and the severity of that harm (CSA Group, 2012, Annex G).
- *Risk analysis:* the systematic use of information to identify hazards and to estimate the risk. Risk analysis provides a basis for risk evaluation and risk control. Information can include current and historical data, theoretical analysis, informed opinions, and the concerns of stakeholders.
- *Risk assessment:* the overall process of risk analysis and risk evaluation. A risk assessment is carried out to find out whether existing control measures prevent harm or more should be done.

Loosely stated, occupational safety management systems are workplace tools and practices established to allow employers to achieve occupational health and safety goals by reducing and managing the risk of workplace illness and injury for employees.

The following steps are frequently involved:

1. Identify the hazards.
2. Decide who might be harmed and how.
3. Evaluate the risks and determine control measures.
4. Record findings made and implement control measures.
5. Review the assessment and update it if necessary.

Safety risk-management principles are as follows:

- Avoid risk wherever possible.
- Carry out a risk assessment to evaluate risks that cannot be avoided.
- Determine and take action to reduce risks to as much as reasonably possible.
- Implement risk-reduction efforts at source wherever possible.

General prevention principles (from Denmark) relate to:

- Prevention of risks;
- Evaluation of risks that cannot be prevented;
- Combating risks at the source;
- Adapting work to the worker, such as with regard to choice of equipment, and limiting monotonous work;
- Replacement of anything hazardous with something that is non-hazardous or less hazardous;

- Planning prevention to make it a cohesive part of the whole, within which prevention covers techniques, organizing work, working conditions, social relationships and the effects of factors in the working environment;
- The adoption of measures for collective protection rather than for individual protection;
- Appropriate instruction of workers. (Arbejdstilsynet, 2020).

Assessing Risk

A risk assessment is conducted to determine the risk (likelihood and consequence of injury or harm to a person) resulting from hazards. It involves identifying what could go wrong—that is, finding what can cause injury or harm to workers, deciding on proper safety control measures to prevent work accidents and occupational diseases, and implementing them using a process such as risk control.

The risk-management process will be implemented in different ways depending on the size and nature of an organization: smaller businesses will manage risks to psychological health in different ways than large businesses. Larger businesses or those where workers are exposed to more, or more serious, psychological health and safety risks may need more complex and sophisticated risk-management processes.

The traditional hierarchy of risk control can involve the following steps:

- Elimination of the hazard;
- Controlling the risk or controlling access to the hazards;
- Substitution of the hazard with something less hazardous;
- Making changes to how the work is organized and done;
- Modifying procedures and practices;
- Administrative/training;
- Protective equipment; and
- Emergency response plans.

Today's Evolving OHS Framework

> There is a general consensus that, in future work scenarios, psychosocial hazards will be more pervasive than traditional occupational safety and health hazards.
>
> (Schulte, 2020)

Psychosocial hazards are coming to be seen as the fourth arm of OHS: biological, chemical, physical, and psychosocial:

> During the last century, many countries across the world have established laws for the prevention of occupational safety and health

(OSH) risks. Generally, these legislative measures have especially taken into account traditional (chemical, physical or biological) risk factors. However, OSH legislation less frequently takes into consideration the so-called "fourth group"—the psychosocial occupational risk factors. Psychosocial hazards (PSH) have been identified as one of the key emerging risks in OSH. They are defined as "those aspects of work design and the organization and management of work, and their social and environmental context, which may have the potential to cause psychological or physical harm." They originate from "interactions between and among work environment, job content, work organization and workers' capacities, needs, culture, personal extra-job considerations that may, through perceptions and experience, influence health, work performance and job satisfaction." Such a broad definition includes countless possible stressors. Occupational or job-related stress is just one of them.

(Chirico et al., 2017, p. 2470)

Psychosocial risks today constitute a major risk for the health and safety of workers, but also for the proper functioning of organizations.

Psychosocial hazards and risks affect both psychological health and safety, and health, safety, and wellbeing at work more broadly. As well as leading to stress, psychosocial risk factors can lead to musculoskeletal disorders:

Psychosocial risks and work-related stress are among the most challenging issues in occupational safety and health. They impact significantly on the health of individuals, organisations and national economies ... when viewed as an organisational issue rather than an individual fault, psychosocial risks and stress can be just as manageable as any other workplace safety and health risk ... When considering the job demands, it is important not to confuse psychosocial risks such as excessive workload with conditions where, although stimulating and sometimes challenging, there is a supportive work environment in which workers are well trained and motivated to perform to the best of their ability.

(European Agency for Safety and Health at Work, 2021)

Risk-management Framework

Psychological health and safety is about applying a risk management framework to psychosocial hazards, and is an increasingly important OHS role due to the need to manage psychosocial risks in a manner consistent with other OHS risks, through an OHS management system and integrated into the organization's broader business processes.

The occupational safety and health profession has a significant contribution to make in preventing the occupational causes of mental ill-health, and is engaged in managing the psychosocial risk of:

• Stress;
• Fatigue;
• Bullying and harassment;
• Violence and aggression.

(IOSH, 2021)

There is a general consensus that, in future work scenarios, psychosocial hazards will be more pervasive than traditional occupational safety and health hazards (3, 11, 16, 17), with profound effects on mental and physical health ... The role of occupational safety and health in the future of work will need to evolve to include a more holistic and public health-oriented approach to addressing worker health (9, 13, 15, 19). Based on a global survey of occupational safety and health professionals (19), it is anticipated that there will be an increase in complexity of health and safety requirements in the future.

(Schulte, 2020)

Risk management as applied to psychosocial hazards is discussed in more detail in Chapter 18.

Psychosocial Hazards in OHS

Psychosocial hazards are not a new topic in the OHS field. A 1984 report from the International Labour Organization (ILO) and the World Health Organization (WHO), first published in 1986, discusses that current trends in the promotion of OHS take into account not only the physical, chemical, and biological hazards in the work environment, but also various psychosocial factors inherent in the enterprise, which may have considerable influence on the physical and mental wellbeing of the worker:

The working environment is increasingly being regarded as a set of interdependent factors making up a complex whole which acts on people at work. The stressful psychosocial factors in the working environment are many and varied. They include physical aspects, some aspects of the organization and system of work, and the quality of human relations in the enterprise. All these factors interact and affect the psychological climate in the enterprise and the physical and mental health of workers.

The concept of psychosocial factors at work is difficult to grasp, since it represents worker perceptions and experience, and reflects many considerations. Some of these considerations relate to the individual worker, while others relate to the conditions of work and the work environment. Still others refer to social and economic influences, which are outside the workplace, but which have repercussions within it.

(International Labour Organization, 1984, pp. 1–3)

Although challenging and often not visible, psychosocial hazards and their potential to result in stress are risks that must be acknowledged and managed in today's OHS realm. Numerous countries outside the United States are already doing this, as discussed in Part II.

References and Further Reading

Arbejdstilsynet. (2020). Preventive measures and general prevention principles, Annex 1 to the Danish Working Environment Authority's Executive Order No. 1406 of 26 September 2020. Available at https://at.dk/en/regulations/execut ive-orders/psychosocial-working-environment-1406/1406-annex-1. Accessed September 22, 2021.

Chirico, F., Heponiemi, T., Pavlova, M., Zaffina, S., & Magnavita, N. (2019). Psychosocial risk prevention in a global occupational health perspective: A descriptive analysis. *International Journal of Environmental Research and Public Health*, 16(14), 2470.

CSA Group. (2012). CSA Z1002: Occupational Health and Safety—Hazard Identification and Elimination and Risk Assessment and Control (Annex G). Available at www.csagroup.org/store/product/2422020. Accessed November 12, 2021.

European Agency for Safety and Health at Work. (2021). Psychosocial risks and stress at work. Available at https://osha.europa.eu/en/themes/psychosocial-risks-and-stress. Accessed July 18, 2021.

Houtman, I. & Jettinghoff, K. (2007). *Raising awareness of stress at work in developing countries A modern hazard in a traditional working environment.* Geneva: World Health Organization. Available at www.who.int/occupational _health/publications/raisingawarenessofstress.pdf. Accessed October 8, 2021.

Institution of Occupational Safety and Health (IOSH). 2021. Psychosocial risks. Available at https://iosh.com/resources-and-research/our-resources/psychosoc ial-risks. Accessed October 12, 2021.

International Labour Organization. (1984). *Psychosocial factors at work: Recognition and control. Report of the Joint ILO/WHO Committee on Occupational Health Ninth Session Geneva, 18–24 September 1984.* Available at www.who.int/occupational_health/publications/ILO_WHO_1984_report_ of_the_joint_committee.pdf. Accessed September 27, 2021.

Schulte, P. A. (2020). A global perspective on addressing occupational safety and health hazards in the future of work. *La Medicina del Lavoro*, 111(3), 163–165.

Chapter 5

More Progress on Psychosocial Hazards Necessary in the United States

Lack of Sufficient Attention to PSH

Government agencies and employers in the United States lag behind many countries and global agencies in their awareness of psychosocial hazards (PHS) and an understanding of their importance in relation to work-related stress.

It is not because U.S. workers do not experience stress at work:

- Nearly 75 percent of U.S. workers report experiencing stress in the workplace (Liu, 2021).
- One-fourth of employees view their jobs as the number one stressor in their lives (Northwestern National Life, 1991).
- Three-fourths of employees believe workers have more on-the-job stress than they did a generation ago. -Princeton Survey Research Associates (CDC, 2014).
- The Centers for Disease Control and Prevention (CDC) state that the mental health of workers is an area of increasing concern to organizations. It found that depression alone leads to more than 200 million lost workdays each year each year, resulting in a cost to employers of between US$17 billion and US$44 billion (CDC, 2016).

Lack of U.S. Data on PSH

The argument that not enough attention is paid to workplace psychosocial hazards in the United States is supported by a 2019 study that "aimed to find out which countries around the world require psychosocial hazards and workplace violence to be assessed by employers through a mandatory occupational risk assessment process and to compare the type of legislation between countries" (Chirico et al., 2019).

The study looked at 132 countries—23 of them considered developed and 109 as developing, according to the United Nations—and determined

DOI: 10.4324/9781003187349-6

that developed countries more frequently had legislatives measures in place. In developed countries, the study generally found "some form of regulations on mental health and/or psychological hazards (psychosocial risks, occupational violence or both of them) in their OSH legislation." (Chirico et al., 2019).

The study stated that, "remarkably, we found 'no data available' from the U.S. with regard to PSH." (Chirico et al., 2019, p. 2470).

This finding does seem remarkable, although it is supported by the following:

> There's been some, but limited, focus on the effects of workplace conditions on employee health and wellbeing, and such emphasis is growing....But for the most part, the emphasis remains on preventing occupational injuries and exposure to hazardous physical conditions, coupled with encouraging health promotion programs, with comparatively limited attention focused on changing the psychosocial dimensions of work that have profound effects on health.
>
> (Pfeffer, 2018, pp. 24–25)

Insights and Oversights: Possibilities for Why the United States Lags Behind on PSH Management

It is difficult to answer why attention to psychosocial hazards in the United States is lagging behind that in other parts of the world. Perhaps it is because the United States only requires a duty of care by the employer for the physical health and safety of employees (discussed below) and not for their psychological health, while many other countries call for this.

Richard Fairfax, retired Deputy Assistant Secretary for OSHA and senior consultant for ORC-NSC states:

> In the U.S. we seem to have gone from strict compliance to behavioral based safety, then to safety and health management systems, and now to HOP and FSI. Psychosocial seems to dance around the perimeter—really not sure why.

He notes that OSHA has been doing business the same way for 50 years now and opines that things have changed and it is time OSHA changes too.

Richard DiNitto, an OHS professional with 40 years' experience in the field, and a founder and principal of The Isosceles Group, a consultancy providing occupational health and safety services to industry and governments worldwide, believes that U.S. employers and organizations disregard workplace psychological health and safety. He opines that this is in part cultural, an extension of a general view in many U.S. workplaces that physical injuries may come from the workplace, but mental ones do not. DiNitto speculates that lack of attention to psychosocial hazards may also stem in part from the OSH Act, which interprets a safe working environment to connote a physical workplace.

Psychosocial Issues Associated with Worker Safety and Health

Europe is clearly ahead of the U.S. in addressing psychosocial issues, and some global companies are beginning to embrace this approach. Psychosocial risks arise from poor work design, organization and management as well as a poor social context of work. These risks may lead to negative psychological, physical and social results such as work-related stress, burnout or depression. There is research that even connects psychosocial factors to an increased risk and incidence of musculoskeletal disorders (MSDs). These are issues on the horizon that OSHA needs to understand and address.

(ORCHSE Strategies LLC, 2021)

Even in the United States, psychological health and safety is not a new topic, but more a stalled one. In 1965, the U.S. National Advisory Environmental Health Committee issued a report to the Surgeon General of the U.S. Public Health Service that foresaw many of the changes that have since occurred in the organization of work. The report highlighted psychological stress as a special concern, noting:

However, three decades have passed and many of these issues still await systematic investigation. What circumstances have stood in the way of more aggressive study of the safety and health consequences of the changing organization of work? To begin with, the subject of organization of work and health has yet to become a cohesive field of study. Numerous disciplines have contributed research on this topic, including labor studies, economics, organizational behavior, public and occupational health, and the job stress field. Presently, little interface exists among these disciplines, and differences exist in methods and endpoints of study.

(CDC, 2002, p. 24)

The report further states that "progress has suffered from too little interchange between the research community and the labor and business communities ... The topic of organization of work needs to be elevated to a higher level of visibility in the occupational safety and health field" (CDC, 2002, pp 24–25).

Limitation: Employer's Duty of Care in the United States Only for Physical Hazards

In the United States, no OHS legislation supports ensuring workplace psychological health and safety; attention is generally only on an employee's physical health and safety.

The Occupational Safety and Health Administration and OSH Act

The mission of the federal Occupational Safety and Health Administration (OSHA) is to ensure that employees work in a safe and healthful environment by setting and enforcing standards, and by providing training, outreach, and assistance. The federal Occupational Health and Safety Act 1970 (OSH Act) covers most private sector employers and their workers, and requires employers to comply with applicable OSHA standards.

Employers must comply with the General Duty Clause of the OSH Act, which requires that all employers provide a work environment "free from recognized hazards that are causing or are likely to cause death or serious physical harm."

Section 5 of the OSH Act states specifically that an employer shall:

- furnish to each of his employees employment and a place of employment which are free from recognized hazards that are causing or are likely to cause death or serious physical harm to his employees;
- comply with occupational safety and health standards promulgated under this Act. (U.S. Department of Labor, 1970)

OSHA recognizes workplace violence as a hazard but does not specifically address psychosocial hazards. OSHA's definition of violence states that:

> Workplace violence is any act or threat of physical violence, harassment, intimidation, or other threatening disruptive behavior that occurs at the work site. It ranges from threats and verbal abuse to physical assaults and even homicide. It can affect and involve employees, clients, customers and visitors.

OSHA advises establishing a zero-tolerance policy toward workplace violence to cover workers, clients, contractors, and anyone else who may come in contact with company personnel. It also suggests that employers assess worksites to identify methods to reduce the likelihood of incidents occurring.

U.S. Federal legislation and OSHA do not specifically address psychosocial hazards and psychological health and safety. This oversight is significant, as many other countries require the employer to ensure both the physical and psychological health and safety of their workers.

However, work-related stress and psychosocial hazards are being addressed in the United States by the National Institute for Occupational Safety and Health (NIOSH) and its Total Worker Health (TWH) program. There is no question that NIOSH and TWH's excellent efforts and progress are increasing the awareness of psychosocial hazards and work-related stress that exists in the United States. These organizations and their work in research and individual organizational interventions are discussed below.

National Institute for Occupational Safety and Health and Total Worker Health

The Occupational Safety and Health (OSH) Act created the National Institute for Occupational Safety and Health (NIOSH), a separate and independent research program to create objective scientific research findings in the field of occupational safety and health. NIOSH's mission is to develop new knowledge in the OHS field and to transfer that knowledge into practice.

Research topics at NIOSH include:

- Characteristics of healthy work organizations;
- Work organization interventions to promote safe and healthy working conditions;
- Monitoring of the changing nature of work;
- Work schedule designs to protect the health and wellbeing of workers;
- Impacts of new organizational policies and practices on worker health and safety; and
- Psychological violence at the workplace.

NIOSH's Worker Wellbeing Questionnaire (WellBQ) offers a free survey instrument that provides an integrated assessment of worker wellbeing. Workers' quality of life, working conditions, circumstances outside of work, and physical and mental health status are addressed. The questionnaire measures worker wellbeing as a holistic construct rather than only workplace or work-related wellbeing.

The WellBQ includes 68 questions covering the five domains of worker wellbeing:

- Work evaluation and experience;
- Workplace policies and culture;
- Workplace physical environment and safety climate;
- Health status;
- Home, community, and society.

The questionnaire also contains 15 optional questions about demographic and employment information.

The NIOSH Job Stress Research Program aims to better understand the influence of work organization and psychosocial factors on stress, illness, and injury, and to identify ways to redesign jobs to create safer and healthier workplaces.

NIOSH's Healthy Work Design and Wellbeing Program

The mission of the Healthy Work Design and Wellbeing (HWD) Cross-Sector Program is to protect and advance worker safety, health, and wellbeing by improving the design of work, management practices, and the physical and psychosocial work environment. HWD partners with industry, labor, trade associations, professional organizations, and academia to better understand how the design of work affects overall health and wellbeing, and how it can be improved to enable workers to thrive and contribute productively at work, at home, and in society (CDC, National Institute for Occupational Safety and Health, 2019).

NIOSH's Total Worker Health Program: An Integrated Approach

NIOSH's Total Worker Health (TWH) program is an emerging concept in occupational safety and health that uses an integrated approach to enhance worker safety, health, and wellbeing. Its policies, programs, and practices integrate protection from work-related safety and health hazards to advance worker wellbeing and optimize workplace culture. Eliminating or reducing recognized hazards in the workplace as the most effective means of prevention is the foundation of the TWH approach.

TWH focuses on an integrated wellbeing strategy, recognizing that wellbeing is affected by multiple factors such as the physical and chemical work environment, psychosocial conditions in the workplace, the home and community environment, and personal health behaviors.

The Hierarchy of Controls Applied to NIOSH Total Worker Health® provides a conceptual model for prioritizing efforts to advance the safety, health, and wellbeing of all workers. It emphasizes organizational-level interventions to protect workers' safety, health, and wellbeing.

There are five steps to apply the Hierarchy of Controls Applied to NIOSH Total Worker Health®:

- First, eliminate workplace conditions that cause or contribute to worker illness and injury, or otherwise negatively impact wellbeing. For example, remove harmful supervisory practices throughout the management chain, if applicable.

- Second, replace unsafe, unhealthy working conditions or practices with safer, health-enhancing policies, programs, and management practices that improve the culture of safety and health in the workplace.
- Third, redesign the work environment, as needed, for improved safety, health, and wellbeing. Examples could include removing barriers to improving wellbeing, enhancing access to employer-sponsored benefits, and providing more flexible work schedules.
- Fourth, provide safety and health education and resources to enhance individual knowledge for all workers.
- Fifth, encourage personal behavior change to improve safety, health, and wellbeing. Assist workers with individual risks and challenges, while providing support in making healthier choices.

(CDC, NIOSH, 2020)

NIOSH Funded Centers of Excellence act as hubs for TWH-related research and practice that build the scientific evidence base necessary to develop new solutions for complex occupational safety and health problems. There are presently ten Centers of Excellence for Total Worker Health.

Other U.S. Agencies and Organizations

The U.S. Equal Employment Opportunity Commission (EEOC) is the federal agency responsible for enforcing federal laws that make it illegal to discriminate against an employee on protected grounds, including sex and accordingly sexual harassment. The EEOC and other state anti-discrimination agencies do not have the legal mandate to regulate workplace psychosocial hazards aside from any role they may play in contributing to status-based discrimination.

Healthy Work Campaign

The Healthy Work Campaign (HWC), a project of the Center for Social Epidemiology, is a public health campaign focused on raising awareness in the United States about the health impacts of work stress on working people. The campaign also focuses on the positive actions that individuals and organizations throughout the U.S. can take to advance healthy work. It serves as a clearinghouse for research and translation of that research into more easily understood resources, accessible tools, and actionable steps to promote healthy work.

Healthy Work Survey

In 2021, the Healthy Work Campaign and researchers developed a survey tool to measure work stressors. The Healthy Work Survey for organizations measures work stressors, also called psychosocial hazards, such as high job demands/workload, supervisor/coworker support, long work hours, low job control, bullying, harassment, and health and safety climate. It is online, free, anonymous, and confidential.

Workplace Bullying Institute

Since 1997, the Workplace Bullying Institute, founded and led by Drs Gary and Ruth Namie, has provided comprehensive, evidence-based, practical solutions for individuals, unions, employers, and lawmakers.

Healthy Workplace Bill

The WBI Healthy Workplace Bill to Prevent & Correct Abuse at Work, drafted by Professor David C. Yamada, was crafted to prevent and correct abusive work environments in U.S. workplaces.

2021 WBI U.S. Workplace Bullying Survey

WBI has periodically commissioned pollster Zogby Analytics to conduct a workplace bullying poll with a representative national sample of adult Americans. Results published in 2021 revealed that over 79 million US workers are affected by workplace bullying, 65 per cent of them by bullying from bosses and 21 percent of them by bullying from coworkers. The remote worker bullying rate was found to be 43 percent.

Coincidence? The United States is an Outlier in Terms of Workplace Bullying Laws

Although 90 percent of adults surveyed in the2021 WBI U.S. Workplace Bullying Survey were in favor of a law against workplace bullying, such as the Healthy Workplace Bill, workplace bullying is generally not illegal in the United States, where workplace bullying generally has no legally recognized legal status or remedy. In plain language, it is legal to bully someone at work so long as this abusive conduct is not based on the target's membership in a protected class such as race, religion, nationality, or disability—known as discrimination.

The United States is one of very few Western countries that has not enacted a law against workplace bullying. In an increasing number of countries, workplace bullying is illegal. In other countries, workplace bullying may not be illegal but codes of practice have been issued by government agencies, which serve as guidance on measures to prevent and address this abusive conduct.

More attention has been brought to workplace bullying in recent years. Still, it is difficult to gage how much, if anything, U.S. employers and employees know about workplace bullying. So here is a quick primer.

- Workplace bullying is cumulative and repeated conduct that may include: false accusations of mistakes and errors; yelling, shouting, and screaming; exclusion and the "silent treatment"; withholding resources and information necessary to do the job; behind-the-back sabotage and defamation; use of put-downs, insults, and excessively harsh criticism; intimidating non-verbal behaviors; and unreasonably heavy work demands.
- Workplace bullying is not: everyday disagreements and "dust-ups" in the office; someone having a bad day and losing their temper; reasonable instructions and directives; and employee reviews.

In Ireland, the Health and Safety Authority states that:

> Bullying is a workplace issue and a human relations issue. Therefore, it comes under the authority of various agencies and is on the agenda of many interested parties. It is a health and safety issue in so far as bullying has been identified as hazardous or dangerous as it can lead to both safety problems and health problems. It is also an IR issue, a HR issue, often a legal issue and a personal and public health issue. So many agencies and interested parties are stakeholders in this difficult area. Employers have a Duty of Care to all employees, to ensure they are both mentally and physically safe at work and that their health is not adversely affected by work. This Duty of Care means employers must behave and react reasonably in relation to such matters.
>
> (Health and Safety Authority, 2021)

Workplace bullying is destructive:

- Workers who witness bullying can have a stronger urge to quit than those who experience it first-hand.
- Workplace bullying, an internal occurrence undertaken by managers and/or coworkers, leads to more workers leaving their jobs than violence, typically inflicted by sources external to a company.

Why U.S. Employers Should Care About Managing Psychosocial Hazards and Work-related Stress

The number of Americans voluntarily quitting their jobs soared to a record high in August 2021, resulting in a record number of job openings and a scarcity of workers (Kellerman, 2021). Workers are experiencing burnout, feeling a lack of engagement with their job and their organization, and frustrated by the lack of support and recognition they receive from their employer. Many are also leaving their jobs for fear of contracting COVID-19 as well as related to managing work–life balance complications brought on by the pandemic (Mutikani, 2021).

Despite the work of NIOSH and TWH, as well as the efforts of the other organizations discussed, U.S. agencies and employers are clearly behind in understanding the importance of managing PSH. It is imperative to bring more attention to this issue to a greater number of U.S. employers, particularly those in OSH, HR, and management.

References and Further Reading

CDC. (2014). STRESS…. at work. National Institute for Occupational Safety and Health. Available at www.cdc.gov/niosh/docs/99-101. Accessed October 27, 2021.

CDC. (2016). Workplace health promotion: Depression evaluation measures. Available at www.cdc.gov/workplacehealthpromotion/health-strategies/depression/evaluation-measures/index.html. Accessed November 1, 2021.

CDC. (2020). NIOSH Total Worker Health® Program. Available at www.cdc.gov/niosh/twh/default.html. Accessed September 23, 2021.

CDC National Institute for Occupational Safety and Health. (2002). *The changing organization of work and the safety and health of working people.* Available at www.cdc.gov/niosh/docs/2002-116/pdfs/2002-116.pdf?id=10.26616/NIOSHPUB2002116. Accessed August 18, 2021.

CDC National Institute for Occupational Safety and Health. (2020). Hierarchy of controls applied to NIOSH Total Worker Health®. Available at www.cdc.gov/niosh/twh/guidelines.html#examples. Accessed September 23, 2021.

CDC National Institute for Occupational Safety and Health. (2013). Stress at work. Available at www.cdc.gov/niosh/topics/stress. Accessed September 23, 2021.

CDC National Institute for Occupational Safety and Health. (2018, March 28). About NIOSH. Available at www.cdc.gov/niosh/about/default.html. Accessed September 23, 2021.

CDC National Institute for Occupational Safety and Health. (2019). Website. Available at www.cdc.gov/niosh. Accessed October 27, 2021.

CDC National Institute for Occupational Safety and Health. (2019). Healthy Work Design and Wellbeing Program. Available at www.cdc.gov/niosh/programs/hwd/description.html. Accessed October 27, 2021.

CDC National Institute for Occupational Safety and Health. (2021). NIOSH Worker Wellbeing Questionnaire (WellBQ). Available at www.cdc.gov/niosh/twh/wellbq/default.html. Accessed September 23, 2021.

Chari, R., Chang, C.-C., Sauter, S. L. … Uscher-Pines, L. (2018). Expanding the paradigm of occupational safety and health: A new framework for worker well-being. *Journal of Occupational and Environmental Medicine*, 60(7), 589–593.

Chirico, F., Heponiemi, T., Pavlova, M., Zaffina, S., & Magnavita, N. (2019). Psychosocial risk prevention in a global occupational health perspective: A descriptive analysis. *International Journal of Environmental Research and Public Health*, 16(14), 2470.

Chirico, F., Heponiemi, T., Pavlova, M., Zaffina, S., & Magnavita, N. (2019). Psychosocial risk prevention in a global occupational health perspective: A descriptive analysis. *International Journal of Environmental Research and Public Health*, 16(14), 2470.

Cobb, E. P. (2017). *Workplace bullying and harassment: New developments in international law*. London: Routledge.

Cunningham, C. J. L. (2020). Psychological and social determinants of health, safety, and well-being at work: The occupational health psychology perspective. Available at www.aiha.org/blog/psychological-and-social-determinants-of-health-safety-and-well-being-at-work-the-occupational-health-psychology-perspective. Accessed September 24, 2021.

DiNitto, R. (2021). Personal Conversation, November 10.

Dobson, M. (2021, September 9). Launch of the Healthy Work Survey for Organizations. Healthy Work Campaign. Available at https://healthywork.org/launch-of-the-healthy-work-survey-for-organizations. Accessed September 20, 2021.

Duffy, M. & Yamada, D. C. (Eds.). (2018). *Workplace bullying and mobbing in the United States*. New York: Praeger.

Health and Safety Authority. (2021). Bullying at work. Available at www.hsa.ie/eng/Workplace_Health/Bullying_at_Work/#Bullying-aHealthandSafetyissue. Accessed October 27, 2021.

Healthy Work Campaign. (2021). Website. Available at https://healthywork.org. Accessed November 14, 2021.

Healthy Workplace Bill. Available at https://healthyworkplacebill.org. Accessed November 14, 2021.

Kellerman, B. (2021, October 12). More Americans are quitting their jobs: Here is how to do it. Reuters. Available at www.reuters.com/business/more-americans-are-quitting-their-jobs-here-is-how-do-it-2021-10-12/?utm_medium=Social&utm_source=twitter. Accessed October 13, 2021.

Liu, J. (2021, June 15). U.S. workers are among the most stressed in the world, new Gallup report finds, CNBC. Available at www.cnbc.com/2021/06/15/gallup-us-workers-are-among-the-most-stressed-in-the-world.html. Accessed September 9, 2021.

Mutikani, L. (2021, October 12). U.S. quits scale record high. Reuters. Available at www.reuters.com/world/us/us-job-openings-fall-still-high-104-million-august-2021-10-12. Accessed October 13, 2021.

Northwestern National Life Insurance Company. (1991). *Employee burnout: America's newest epidemic*. Minneapolis, MN: Northwestern National Life Insurance Company.

ORCHSE Strategies LLC. (2021). *OSHA White Paper*. Available at www.orchse-strategies.com/wp-content/uploads/OSHA-WHITE-PAPER-FINAL.2.22.21-.pdf. Accessed September 23, 2021.

Pfeffer, J. (2018). *Dying for a paycheck: How modern management harms employee health and company performance—and what we can do about it.* New York: HarperBusiness.

U.S. Department of Labor. (1970). *OSH Act of 1970.* Available at www.osha.gov/laws-regs/oshact/completeoshact. Accessed October 27, 2021.

U.S. Department of Labor, OSHA. (2021). Workplace violence. Available at www.osha.gov/workplace-violence. Accessed November 3, 2021.

WBI. (2021). *U.S. Workplace Bullying Survey.* Available at https://workplacebullying.org/2021-wbi-survey-infographic. Accessed September 23, 2021.

Workplace Bullying Institute. Website. Available at https://workplacebullying.org. Accessed October 27, 2021.

Part II

International Insights and Examples

Part II explores measures taken by other countries and globally to identify, assess, and address psychosocial hazards around the world. Specific examinations of mandatory and non-mandatory psychosocial risk management in Europe as a whole, a number of European countries, Mexico, Canada, Australia, Japan, and in a global context are included.

DOI: 10.4324/9781003187349-7

Chapter 6

Management of Psychosocial Hazards in Europe

Work-related Stress and Psychosocial Hazards in Europe

Many Europeans experience stress from work:

> A European opinion poll conducted by EU-OSHA shows that about a half of workers consider the problem with work-related stress to be common in their workplace. Among the most frequently mentioned causes of work-related stress are job reorganisation or job insecurity, working long hours or excessive workload, and harassment and violence at work.
>
> (EU-OSHA, 2021)

> Already before the pandemic, mental health problems affected about 84 million people in the EU. Half of EU workers consider stress to be common in their workplace, and stress contributes to around half of all lost working days. Nearly 80% of managers are concerned about work-related stress. As a result of the pandemic, close to 40% of workers began to work remotely full time. This blurs the traditional boundaries between work and private life and together with other remote-working trends, such as permanent connectivity, a lack of social interaction, and increased use of ICT, has given and additional rise to psychosocial and ergonomic risks.
>
> (EUR-Lex, 2021)

In Europe, 25 per cent of workers say they experience work-related stress for all or most of their time at work, and a similar proportion report that work affects their health negatively. Psychosocial risks contribute to these adverse effects of work. The most common risks relate to the types of tasks workers perform—for example, whether tasks are monotonous or complex—and to work intensity. High work intensity is associated with negative health and wellbeing outcomes, especially work-related stress.

DOI: 10.4324/9781003187349-8

Violence and harassment are less frequently reported but have a strong negative relationship with wellbeing. Other working conditions, such as a good work–life balance and social support, have a positive influence.

Psychosocial risks are of concern to a majority of companies, with nearly 80 percent of managers expressing concern about work-related stress, and nearly one in five considering violence and harassment to be major concerns. Looking at single risks, managers' greatest concerns relate to time pressure and difficult customers, patients, and pupils. Despite these concerns, fewer than one-third of establishments have procedures in place to deal with such risks.

Evidence suggests that tackling hazards to psychosocial wellbeing is not a single event, but a process with different stages that require changes in the work environment. Interventions at company level are best implemented through a structured process, and this is most successful if accompanied by active worker involvement (Eurofound, 2014).

Concern over psychosocial risks increases as the size of the establishment grows. Work-related stress is reported to be of some or major concern in around 90 percent of large establishments (with 250 and more employees) and in 75 percent of the smallest establishments (with 10–19 employees) (Eurofound, 2014).

The Employer's Duty of Care

In many European countries, the employer's duty of care is regarded as encompassing both the physical and psychological aspects of work. Legislation has established that the European employer's duty of care for workers extends to psychological as well as physical worker health and safety pursuant to EU Directive 89/391/EEC Framework Directive on Occupational Health and Safety.

Psychosocial risk management is among the responsibilities of employers as stipulated in EU Directive 89/391/EEC Framework Directive on Occupational Health and Safety (Directive 89/391/EEC),[1] which introduces measures to encourage improvements in the safety and health of workers at work and lays down employers' general obligations to ensure workers' health and safety, stating that employers have a duty to ensure the safety and health of workers in every aspect related to their work.

Employers are obliged to address and manage all types of risk in a preventive manner and to establish health and safety procedures and systems to do so. A number of policies and guidance of relevance to psychosocial risk management have been developed on the basis of this Directive, and are applicable at European level (Milczarek & Irastorza, 2021).

The European Agency for Safety and Health at Work (EU-OSHA) holds the position that Directive 89/391/EEC on safety and health of workers at work lays down the employer's general obligations to ensure workers' health and safety in every aspect related to work, including psychosocial risks. It states that psychosocial risks can be assessed and managed in the same systematic way as traditional workplace risks (European Agency for Safety and Health at Work, 2014).

There is also the recognition, reflected in European legislation, that one component of health and safety at work is taking a worker's dignity into consideration. The concept of a worker's dignity is provided for in the European Union's Bill of Rights, the Charter of Fundamental Rights of the European Union, which states that every worker has the right to working conditions that respect their health, safety, and dignity. The term dignity is included in the language of numerous EU laws on bullying, harassment, and sexual harassment. Workplace bullying is a clear violation of dignity.

Relevant EU Legislative and Non-legislative Instruments and Surveys

In addition to the European Union's Framework Directive on Occupational Health and Safety, a number of relevant Framework Agreements and surveys address management of psychosocial hazards.

A Focus on Psychosocial Risks

For close to 20 years, EU-OSH strategic frameworks have played a pivotal role in the way national authorities and social partners decide on OSH objectives.

The EU Strategic Framework on Health and Safety at Work 2021–2027 Occupational Safety and Health, adopted by the European Commission on June 28, 2021, includes a call for a focus on psychosocial risks.

The Europe Commission proclaimed that it would do the following:

- Launch an "EU-OSHA healthy workplaces campaign" 2023–2025 on creating a safe and healthy digital future covering psychosocial and ergonomic risks in particular;
- In cooperation with Member States and social partners,[2] prepare a non-legislative EU-level initiative related to mental health at work that assesses emerging issues related to workers' mental health and puts forward guidance for action before the end of 2022;
- Develop the analytical basis, e-tools and guidance for risk assessments related to green and digital jobs and processes, including in particular psychosocial and ergonomic risks;
- Ensure appropriate follow-up to the European Parliament Resolution on the right to disconnect. (Eur-Lex, 2021)

The EU Framework Agreement on Work-related Stress

The framework agreement on work-related stress (Agreement), 2004, clarifies the relevance of Directive 89/391/EEC for the management of work-related stress and psychosocial risks. The non-binding agreement's objective is to provide employers and employees with a framework of measures that will identify and prevent the problems of work-related stress and help manage them when they do arise. It aims for employees and employers to work together at better identifying, preventing, and managing stress, and to take action accordingly. The responsibility for determining the appropriate measures rests with the employer.

Key provisions of the agreement include:

- Acknowledging stress as a common concern of European employers, workers, and their representatives;
- Inclusion of work-related stress and its causal factors among the risks that should be prevented;
- Laying down a general framework for preventing, eliminating and managing stressors, with specific reference to work organization, work content, and the working environment;
- Setting forth the employer's responsibility and emphasizing participation and cooperation by workers and their representatives in the practical implementation of measures to reduce stress as essential;
- Taking into account stress that does not stem from the workplace or working conditions if it creates stress inside the workplace.

Recently, the European Trade Union Institute (ETUI) called for an EU Directive in the area of psychosocial risks in the workplace:

> The exposures to psychosocial work factors are modifiable by preventive policies that address work organisation and working and employment conditions. The ETUC is calling for an EU Directive in the area of psychosocial risks in the workplace, as the implementation of the 2004 autonomous framework agreement on work-related stress in the Member States remains patchy, and the scope of worker protection inadequate....Further, the degree to which psychosocial risks are included or explicitly mentioned in the legislation varies significantly between the Member States, and consequently, workers are not protected to the same level across the countries.
>
> (ETUI, 2021)

Framework Agreement on Harassment and Violence at Work

The Framework Agreement on Harassment and Violence at Work (European Agency for Safety and Health at Work, 2004) aims to increase awareness and understanding of workplace harassment and violence among employees, workers, and their representatives, and to provide employers, workers, and their representatives at all levels with an action-oriented framework to identify, manage, and prevent problems of harassment and violence at work.

Practical e-Guide to Managing Psychosocial Risks

An e-guide to managing stress and psychosocial risks at work(EU-OSHA 2014) is particularly intended for people working in micro and small enterprises. Information is provided for employers—especially those employing fewer than 50 workers—about work-related stress and psychosocial risks, and their causes and consequences. The goal is to improve general understanding and awareness of these issues in the workplace.

The e-guide is designed to respond to the needs of organizations that are starting to approach psychosocial risks in the workplace. It provides guidance on initial steps, including simple explanations of work-related stress and psychosocial risks and their effects on businesses and workers, as well as practical examples of how to prevent and deal with psychosocial risks.

European Survey of Enterprises on New and Emerging Risks

EU-OSHA's European Survey of Enterprises on New and Emerging Risks (ESENER) is a periodic extensive survey that looks at how European workplaces manage safety and health risks in practice, with a particular focus on psychosocial risks (European Agency for Safety and Health at Work, 2019).

The Third European Survey of Enterprises on New and Emerging Risks, conducted in 2019, asked those "who know best about health and safety in the establishments" about the way health and safety risks are managed in their workplace, including the main drivers of and barriers to effective management and worker participation, with a particular focus on psychosocial risks, such as work-related stress, violence, and harassment. A total of 45,420 establishments were surveyed across 33 European countries.

A questionnaire sought information on four areas of OSH:

- The general approach in the establishment to managing OSH;
- How the "emerging" area of psychosocial risks is addressed;
- The main drivers of and barriers to the management of OSH;
- How worker participation in OSH management occurs in practice.

Establishments reported that psychosocial risk factors are more difficult to manage than other OSH risks. A reluctance to talk openly about these issues appeared to be the main difficulty when it came to addressing psychosocial risks (61 percent of establishments in the EU-28).

Notes

1   A European Union (EU) Directive is a legal act provided for in an EU Treaty. EU Directives are legally binding and have to be transposed into national laws by member states within a set deadline. EU Directives set out minimum requirements and fundamental principles, such as the principle of prevention and risk assessment, as well as the responsibilities of employers and employees. A directive enters into force once it is published in the Official Journal of the European Union. EU member states are free to adopt stricter rules for the protection of workers when transposing EU directives into national law; accordingly, legislative requirements can vary across EU member states.

2   The European social partners are the bodies representing the two sides of industry: the employers and the employees. The ETUC is the only organization authorized to speak on behalf of workers and their representatives at European level. On the employers' side there are three: BUSINESSEUROPE (private firms), UEAPME (small businesses) and CEEP (public employers). The ETUC is the voice of workers and represents 45 million members from 90 trade union organizations in 38 European countries, plus 10 European Trade Union Federations (European Trade Union Confederation (ETUC), n.d.).

References and Further Reading

ETUI. (2021). Evidence is strong on negative health effects of psychosocial work factors. Available at www.etui.org/news/evidence-strong-negative-health-effects-psychosocial-work-factors. Accessed October 31, 2021.

EU-OSHA. (2004). *The EU Framework Agreement on Work-Related Stress.* Available at https://osha.europa.eu/en/legislation/guidelines/framework-agreement-work-related-stress. Accessed November 2, 2021.

EU-OSHA. (2021). Psychosocial risks and stress at work. Available at https://osha.europa.eu/en/news/managing-workplace-stress-by-tackling-harassment-and-bullying. Accessed November 12, 2021.

EUR-Lex. (2007). Directive 2007/30/ EC, amending Council Directive 89/391/EEC. Available at http://eur-lex.europa.eu/legal-content/EN/ALL/?uri=CELEX:32007L0030. Accessed September 20, 2021.

EUR-Lex. (1989). Directive 89/391/EEC. Available at http://eur-lex.europa.eu/legal-content/EN/TXT/?uri=CELEX:01989L0391-20081211. Accessed September 23, 2021.

EUR-Lex. (2021). *EU strategic framework on health and safety at work 2021–2027: Occupational safety and health in a changing world of work.* Available at https://eur-lex.europa.eu/legal-content/ EN/TXT/?uri=CELEX%3A520 21DC0323&qid=1626089672913#PP1Contents. Accessed July 18, 2021.

Eurofound. (2014). *Psychosocial risks in Europe: Prevalence and strategies for prevention.* Available at www.eurofound.europa.eu/publications/report/2014/eu-member-states/working-conditions/psychosocial-risks-in-europe-prevalence-and-strategies-for-prevention. Accessed June 15, 2021

European Agency for Safety and Health at Work. (2014). E-guide to managing stress and psychosocial risks. Available at https://osha.europa.eu/en/tools-and-resources/e-guides/e-guide-managing-stress-and-psychosocial-risks. Accessed September 9, 2021.

European Agency for Safety and Health at Work. (2019). How European workplaces manage safety and health. Available at https://visualisation.osha.europa.eu/esener#!/en/survey/overview/2019. Accessed September 23, 2021.

European Agency for Safety and Health at Work. (2021). Psychosocial risks and stress at work. Available at: http://osha.europa.eu/en/topics/stress/index_html/violence. Accessed September 24, 2021.

European Agency for Safety and Health at Work. (2004). *Framework Agreement on Work-related Stress*. Available at https://osha.europa.eu/en/legislation/guidelines/framework-agreement-on-work-related-stress. Accessed September 9, 2021.

European Agency for Safety and Health at Work. (2014). *Healthy workplaces manage stress: Campaign guide – managing stress and psychosocial risks at work*. Available at https://data.europa.eu/doi/10.2802/16611. Accessed October 31, 2021.

European Agency for Safety and Health at Work. (2017). *Framework Agreement on Harassment and Violence at Work*. Available at https://osha.europa.eu/en/legislation/guidelines/framework-agreement-on-harassment-and-violence-at-work. Accessed September 23, 2021.

European Agency for Safety and Health at Work. (2019). Third European Survey of Enterprises on New and Emerging Risks 2019 (ESENER-3). Available at https://osha.europa.eu/en/publications/third-european-survey-enterprises-new-and-emerging-risks-esener-3#:~:text=EU%2DOSHA's%20Third%20European%20Survey,work%2Drelated%20stress%2C%20violence%20and. Accessed September 23, 2021.

European Foundation for the Improvement of Living and Working Conditions (Eurofound) and European Agency for Safety and Health at Work. (2014). *Psychosocial risks in Europe: Prevalence and strategies for prevention*. Available at www.eurofound.europa.eu/publications/report/2014/eu-member-states/working-conditions/psychosocial-risks-in-europe-prevalence-and-strategies-for-prevention. pp. 42–44 Accessed June 15, 2021.

European Trade Union Confederation (ETUC). (n.d.). Who are the European social partners? Available at www.etuc.org/en/who-are-european-social-partners. Accessed November 17, 2021.

Milczarek, M. & Irastorza, X. (2021). *Drivers and barriers for psychosocial risk management: An analysis of the findings of the European Survey of Enterprises on New and Emerging Risks (ESENER) Report*. Available at https://osha.europa.eu/en/publications/drivers-and-barriers-psychosocial-risk-management-analysis-findings-european-survey (Accessed November 20, 2021).

Chapter 7

Nordic Countries and Belgium

Psychosocial Hazards as an Umbrella Term

Nordic Countries

A number of Nordic countries use psychosocial hazards (PSH) as an umbrella term, addressing all PSHs in one law rather than enacting separate laws, such as on bullying or on sexual harassment, with the general objective of regulating work-related stress and ensuring employees' psychological health and safety.

Nordic countries were among the first to include psychosocial factors in risk assessments of working conditions (International Labour Organization, 2016. Pp 1–2 Workplace Stress a Collective Challenge)

Sweden and Denmark: Collaboration Between Employer and Employee

Sweden

Swedish legislation on the Work Environment regulates psychological and social aspects of the work environment. Sweden's Work Environment Authority states: "Our mental and social work environment is just as important as the physical" (Swedish Work Environment Authority, 2016). Cooperation between employer and employee is emphasized:

Psychosocial work environment responsibilities that became effective in 2016 clarified an employer's responsibilities for the psychosocial work environment. The regulations are part of laws imposing on employers an obligation to continuously review and manage the working environment.

Employees also have responsibilities:

> The basic idea is that the employer and employee shall co-operate. This means that both of them should actively seek contact with each other with the purpose of establishing a good working environment;

DOI: 10.4324/9781003187349-9

among other things they must consider mental risks. Every employer is obligated to take all precautions possible against the occurrence of sickness or accidents, including psychological injuries.

(Steinberg, 2017, pp. 106)

The participation of the employee is seen as important for psychological wellbeing in the workplace:

Working conditions shall be adapted to people's differing physical and mental aptitudes. This adaptation shall consider differences due to sex, age, and degree of experience. Different psychological needs must also be taken into account. The employee shall be given the opportunity of participating in the design of his own work situation and in processes of change and development affecting his own work.

(Steinberg, 2017, pp. 107)

Denmark: Executive Order on the Psychosocial Work Environment

As with Sweden, Danish law calls for collaboration between employer, supervisors, and employees. The law states that the safety and health work in the individual company is handled through cooperation between the employer, the supervisors, and the other employees.

The Executive Order on Psychosocial Work Environment is Denmark's first executive order on the psychosocial work environment. It concerns the psychosocial working environment and contains detailed rules supplementing working environment legislation (Ministry of Employment, 2020). It is seen as progress in the fight for a better mental work environment.

The Executive Order forms an important foundation for ensuring real equality between the physical and mental work environment, and applies to any work performed for an employer. It requires that the workplace "must be designed with attention to health and safety, both individually and collectively in terms of way the psychosocial working environment may impact on physical or psychosocial health in both short and long term" (Danish Working Environment Authority, 2020). The Order does the following:

- Establishes that it is always the employer's responsibility to organize the work in such a way that it can be carried out in a safe and healthy manner in relation to influences in the mental work environment. It does not contain new requirements for companies.

- Defines the impact on the psychosocial working environment as the psychosocial effects of the work that takes place in relation to the following:
  - The way the work is planned and organized;
  - Organizational conditions of importance to the work carried out by the employees;
  - The content of the work, including the requirements of the work;
  - The way the work is performed;
  - The social relations in the workplace.

The Danish Working Environment Authority intends to supplement the executive order with three guidelines for organizations on large workloads and time pressures; unclear requirements and conflicting demands at work; and high emotional demands in working with people. Guidelines already exist on violence and abusive acts, including bullying and sexual harassment.

Annex I to Executive Order: Preventive Measures and General Prevention Principles

Annex 1 to The Danish Working Environment Authority's Executive Order No. 1406 of 26 September 2020 on the psychosocial working environment lists examples of preventative measures that impact the psychosocial environment:

- Responsible planning and organization of the work;
- Adequate and appropriate training and instruction in carrying out the work;
- Effective supervision of the work;
- Proper design of the work site;
- Correct use of technical aids that must be suitable for, or adapted to, the work;
- Possibility for support in the work, including managerial and collegial support;
- Possibility of influence in relation to the work to be performed.

Norway

Norway's Working Environment Act covers the psychosocial work environment. The Act relates to working environment, working hours and employment protection, among other areas (Working Environment Act No. 62/2005, as amended), and covers the psychosocial work environment. The employer is responsible for ensuring that the working environment is fully satisfactory regarding employees' physical and mental health and welfare, and for ensuring equality.

The purpose of the Act is to:

- Secure a working environment that provides a basis for a healthy and meaningful working situation, that affords full safety from harmful physical and mental influences and that has a standard of welfare at all times consistent with the level of technological and social development of society;
- Ensure sound conditions of employment and equality of treatment at work;
- Facilitate a satisfactory climate for expression in the undertaking;
- Facilitate adaptations of the individual employee's working situation in relation to their capabilities and circumstances of life;
- Provide a basis whereby the employer and the employees of undertakings may themselves safeguard and develop their working environment in cooperation with the employers' and employees' organizations and with the requisite guidance and supervision of the public authorities;
- Foster inclusive working conditions (Lovdata, 2006).

General requirements regarding the working environment in Norway contain the following considerations:

- The working environment shall be fully satisfactory in terms of factors that may influence employees' physical and mental health and welfare. The standard of safety, health, and working environment shall be continuously developed and improved in accordance with developments in society.
- When planning and arranging the work, emphasis shall be placed on preventing injuries and diseases. The organization, arrangement, and management of work, working hours, pay systems, including use of performance-related pay, technology, and so on shall be arranged in such a way that means the employees are not exposed to adverse physical or mental strain and that due regard is paid to safety considerations.
- Further requirements for the psychosocial work environment in the Act include the following:
  - The work shall be arranged so that employees' integrity and dignity are safeguarded.
  - Efforts should be made to arrange work so that it provides the opportunity for contact and communication with other workers in the organization.

- Employees shall not be subjected to harassment or other improper conduct.
- An employee shall, as far as possible, be protected from violence, threats, and adverse impact as a result of contact with others. (Lovdata, 2006)

The Netherlands

Legislation on working conditions in the Netherlands refers to psycho-social workload (PSA), or psychosocial pressure, a reference to stress.

Factors that influence PSA and may cause stress include:

- Aggression and violence;
- Labor discrimination;
- Bullying;
- Sexual harassment;
- Workload.

Dutch laws on working conditions call upon the employer to operate a policy aimed at preventing employment-related psychosocial pressure, or limiting it if prevention is not possible, as part of the general working conditions policy. The employer is also required to conduct a risk assessment with regard to psychosocial pressures in the workplace and adopt an action plan.

Belgium

All psychosocial risks that could lead to stress are incorporated into the general framework of legislation regulating psychosocial risks at work in Belgium. Rather than being limited to harassment, violence, and sexual harassment, legislation places these topics in the more general framework of psychosocial risks, which include stress, conflicts, and burnout.

Psychosocial risks at work are defined as the probability that one or more workers will suffer psychological damage, which may also be accompanied by physical damage, following exposure to components of the work organization, the content of the work, working conditions, and interpersonal relationships at work, on which the employer has an impact, and which objectively entail a danger. Stress, moral harassment, burnout, suicide, and alcohol and drug abuse are specified as the best-known manifestations of psychosocial risks.

Psychosocial risks related to work cover occupational risks that affect both the mental and physical health of workers, and that have an impact on the proper functioning and performance of companies, as well as on safety. The origin of these risks lies in the organization of work, work content, working conditions, working life conditions, and interpersonal relationships at work.

Belgian law on prevention of psychosocial risks at work calls for the role of a person of trust, or "prevention advisor psychosocial aspects' as part of an internal department to assist the employer, management, and employees in the implementation of measures related to the wellbeing of workers.

Belgium's Federal Public Service for Employment, Labor and Social Dialogue states that psychosocial risks are complex because their origins are multifactorial, and the dangers can be found at several levels. The origin of these risks lies in working conditions and work organization, as specified below:

- Work organization includes the organizational structure (horizontal-vertical), the way the tasks are distributed, the work procedures, the management tools, the management style, the general policies implemented.
- The content of the work is the workers' tasks, including everything relating to the complexity and variation of tasks, emotional requirements (relationship with the public, contact with suffering, etc.), mental load (linked, among other things, to the difficulty of task), physical load, and task clarity.
- Working conditions include types of contracts and schedules, the possibilities of learning, and the physical environment in which the work is performed, such as the layout of the workplace, work equipment, noise, and work positions.
- Interpersonal relations at work include internal relations between workers and with managers, but also relations with third parties. (Federal Public Service for Employment, Labor and Social Dialogue, 2021).

The employer must take necessary measures to prevent psychosocial risks at work to prevent damage arising from these risks or to limit such damage.

Belgian legislation requires that the employer identify situations that can lead to psychosocial risks at work, determine and assess these risks, and determine which measures must be taken to prevent them, taking into account the nature of the activities and the size of the enterprise, as well as hazards of the components of work organization, job content, working conditions, conditions of work life, and interpersonal relationships at work.

The risk analysis on psychosocial risks at work is carried out by the employer with employee participation.

Belgian Tools and Guides

Psychosocial Risk at Work Alert Indicators Tool

The Federal Public Service's *Psychosocial Risk at Work Alert Indicators*, updated in June 2020, is a tool used to pre-diagnose psychosocial risks and alert employers to their presence within the company. The "psychosocial risk warning indicators" can be used in all companies and organizations, regardless of their sector of activity.

Guide to the Prevention of Psychosocial Risks at Work

The purpose of this guide is to help organisations and companies— including SMEs and very small enterprises—to adopt and pursue a policy to prevent psychosocial risks that sits within a more general policy on the management of professional risks as well as within social dialogue. The possible solutions put forward recommend collective measures which take account of the organisation of the work."

(Federal Public Service for Employment, Labor and
Social Dialogue, 2016)

In sum, Nordic countries' laws on psychosocial hazards, as well as Belgium's general legislative framework for psychosocial risks, including stress, conflicts, and burnout, recognize the importance of managing psychological health and safety. Their incorporation of an employer's duty of care for psychological as well as physical risks offers an important approach to today's work environment.

References and Further Reading

Arbejdstilsynet (2020). *Annex 1 to The Danish Working Environment Authority's Executive Order No. 1406 of 26 September 2020*. Available at https://at.dk/en/regulations/executive-orders/psychosocial-working-environment-1406/1406-annex-1. Accessed September 23, 2021.

Cobb, E. P. (2017). *Workplace bullying and harassment: New developments in international law*. London: Routledge.

Danish Working Environment Authority (2020. *Executive Order No. 1406 of 26 September 2020 on psychosocial working environment*. Available at https://at.dk/en/regulations/executive-orders/psychosocial-working-environment-1406. Accessed September 13, 2021

Federal Public Service Employment Labor and Social Dialogue. (2021). Psychosocial risks at work: Definitions and scope. Available at https://emploi.belgique.be/fr/themes/bien-etre-au-travail/risques-psychosociaux-au-travail/definitions-et-champ-dapplication. Accessed September 27, 2021.

Federal Public Service for Employment, Labor and Social Dialogue. (2016). *Guide to the prevention of psychosocial risks at work.* Available at https:// employment.belgium.be/sites/default/files/content/publications/PSR_Guide_prevention_EN_2020.pdf. Accessed October 8, 2021.

Federal Public Service for Employment, Labor and Social Dialogue, Psychosocial Risks. (n.d.). Available at www.beswic.be/fr/themes/risques-psychosociaux-rps. Accessed October 8, 2021.

Federal Public Service for Employment, Labor and Social Dialogue. (2020). Psychosocial risks: Update of the tool "Warning indicators for psychosocial risks at work." Available at https://emploi.belgique.be/fr/actualites/mise-jour-de-loutil-indicateurs-dalerte-des-risques-psychosociaux-au-travail. Accessed October 8, 2021.

International Labour Organization. (2016). Workplace stress: A collective challenge. Available at www.ilo.org/safework/info/publications/WCMS_466 547/lang--en/index.htm. Accessed November 3, 2021.

Lovdata. (2006). Act Relating to Working Environment, Working Hours and Employment Protection, etc. (Working Environment Act). Available at https:// lovdata.no/dokument/NLE/lov/2005-06-17-62#KAPITTEL_4. Accessed September 21, 2021.

Ministry of Employment. (2020). Progress in the fight for a better mental work environment. Available at https://bm.dk/nyheder-presse/pressemeddelelser/ 2020/09/fremskridt-i-kampen-for-bedre-psykisk-arbejdsmiljoe. Accessed November 9, 2021.

Ministry of Employment. (2020). Progress in the fight for a better mental work environment. Available at https://bm.dk/nyheder-presse/pressemeddelelser/ 2020/09/fremskridt-i-kampen-for-bedre-psykisk-arbejdsmiljoe. Accessed November 9, 2021.

Ministry of Justice. (2014). *Royal Decree of 10 April 2014 on Prevention of Psychosocial Risks at Work.* Available at www.ejustice.just.fgov.be/ cgi_loi/change_lg.pl?language=fr&la=F&table_name=loi&cn=2014041013. Accessed October 8, 2021.

Retsinformation. (2020). *Executive Order on Mental Work Environment at BEK No. 1406 of 26/09/2020.* Available at www.retsinformation.dk/eli/lta/ 2020/1406#ide1e902d1-b980-4043-9f04-f0ac9a25e874. Accessed September 23, 2021.

Retsinformation. (2021). Denmark's executive order on competence injunctions. Available at www.retsinformation.dk/eli/lta/2021/354. Accessed November 3, 2021.

Steinberg, M. (2017). Strength and weakness of the Swedish legislation regarding psychosocial risks. In L. Lerouge (Ed.), *Psychosocial risks in labour and social security law: A cooperative legal overview from Europe, North America, Australia and Japan* (pp. 105–121). New York: Springer.

Swedish Work Environment Authority. (2016). Website. Available at www.av.se/ en. Accessed November 16, 2021.

Chapter 8

Work–Life Balance

Work-life balance, also known as work–life interface, is defined generally as the equilibrium between personal life and work life, and is a psychosocial hazard. Research suggests that poor work–life balance is associated with poor health outcomes, including psychological strain, depression, burnout, and stress.

The Right to Disconnect

The right to disconnect refers to an employee's right to be able to disengage from work and refrain from engaging in work-related electronic communications, such as emails, telephone calls, or other messages, outside normal working hours.

In today's world of work, particularly during the COVID-19 pandemic, the lines have become blurred between being "at work" and "not at work," due to the constant connection to mobile devices and the rapid rise in remote work.

The constant connection can be beneficial, but also carries health risks for employees when it is not balanced against the need for rest. Understanding the negative effects of being constantly connected continues to evolve, and can include risks such as anxiety, depression, and burnout.

The issue of the "right to disconnect" emerged in France, which in January 2017 became the first country to enact a law in response to concerns that mobile technologies had negative impacts on work–life balance. The French Labor Code requires all companies with 50 employees or more to reach an agreement with workers' representatives regulating the use of digital devices during rest and leave periods. Portugal, Spain, and Italy have also enacted versions of a right to disconnect law.

Currently, no EU legislation specifically addresses the right to disconnect. However, in January 2021 the European Parliament adopted a

DOI: 10.4324/9781003187349-10

resolution calling on the European Commission to propose legislation on the right to disconnect.

Argentina and Peru have also enacted laws on the right to disconnect. Ontario has also enacted legislation which includes a host of measures for workers, including right-to-disconnect policies.

Ireland's Code of Practice on Right to Disconnect

Ireland's Workplace Relations Commission Code of Practice for Employers and Employees on the Right to Disconnect (Code)[1] became effective on April 1, 2021. The Code's purpose is to provide practical guidance and best practice to organizations, employees, and their representatives in relation to the right to disconnect. It is applicable to all types of employment, whether office-based, working remotely, or as a mobile worker.

The Code was established to address the concern that employees "are always contactable and accessible" due to technological advances in recent years, and sets out a right for employees to disconnect or switch off from their roles outside of normal working hours.

The foreword to Ireland's 2021 Code captures it well:

> The world of work has changed profoundly over recent years. Technological advances mean that we are always contactable and accessible. Where, when and how we work continues to change at an accelerating pace. Employers and employees are experiencing both challenges and benefits arising from new ways of working including remote and flexible working arrangements, which encapsulates how long, where, and at what times employees work as well as the location of where work gets done ... While different working arrangements may suit different employees within their respective business environments, the right to be able to maintain clear boundaries between work and leisure is universal.
>
> (Workplace Relations Commission, 2021)

The Code has three main objectives:

- The right of an employee to not routinely perform work outside of normal working hours;
- The right to not be penalized for refusing to attend to work matters outside of normal working hours; and
- The duty to respect another person's right to disconnect by, for example, not routinely emailing or calling outside normal working hours.

The Code states that employers should develop a right to disconnect policy,

> having engaged with their employees and/or trade union or employees' representatives, which, once finalized, should be widely communicated within an organization. While emphasis should be placed on the right of employees to disconnect outside of normal working hours and on annual leave, the Code recognizes the reality that legitimate reasons may exist for occasionally having to contact employees outside of normal working hours. A balance should be sought in terms of flexibility to ensure both an employer and employees needs are met.
>
> Where appropriate, the Policy should recognize that certain businesses and roles within those businesses do not always operate on a standard hours basis but in a manner responsive to customer needs where flexibility is required to meet the needs of the business, and as agreed in the employee's terms of employment. In this regard, the Policy should recognise that such flexibility may be beneficial also to employees and a Policy should find the appropriate balance in terms of employer and employee outcomes.
>
> (Workplace Relations Commission, 2021)

Both employers and employees have obligations. Employer obligations include the following:

- Provide detailed information in relation to employees' working times;
- Detail employees' normal working hours or the hours they would reasonably be expected to work;
- Ensure employees take appropriate rest periods;
- Ensure a safe workplace;
- Ensure no penalization occurs where an employee acts in compliance with a relevant provision or performs any duty or exercises any right under section 27 of the Safety Health and Welfare at Work Act, 2005.

Employee obligations include the following:

- Manage their own work time and to take reasonable care to protect their own safety, health and welfare, in addition to the health and safety of co-workers;
- Cooperate fully with any appropriate mechanism utilized by an employer to record working time, including when working remotely;
- Be mindful of their colleagues, customers, clients and other people's rights to disconnect;

- Notify the employer in writing of any statutory rest break or period to which they were entitled and which they were not able to avail themselves of on a particular occasion, with the reason for not having taken such a rest period or break;
- Be conscious of their work pattern and aware of their work-related wellbeing, and take remedial action if necessary.

Spain's Law on Remote Work

Spain's decree to regulate remote working became effective in October 2021. These new regulations were negotiated between the government, unions, and business associations. For the regulations to apply, an employee must work at least 30 percent of their total hours remotely within a period of three months, which equals one and a half days a week.

There is a difference between remote work and telework:

- Remote work is a form of organization of work or of carrying out the work activity provided at the home of the worker or in a place chosen by them, during all or part of their working day, on a regular basis;
- Telework is work done at a distance that is carried out through the exclusive or prevalent use of computer, telematic and telecommunication means and systems.

Teleworking is voluntary for both the employer and employee; the organization and worker must sign a written agreement before the remote working begins. The employee has 10 days to deliver this text to their representatives, who need to submit it to the employment office.

The following is the mandatory minimum content of the distance work agreement:

- Details of means, equipment, and tools required for remote working;
- A list of the expenses that the employee may incur due to working from home and how these will be met by the company;
- Employee's working hours and availability;
- Percentage and distribution of face-to-face versus remote working;
- The office address to which the employee is assigned and where, if applicable, they will perform any face-to-face part of the working day;
- The location where the employee will work remotely (their address);
- How the company and the employee may terminate or reverse the home working agreement;
- Details of how the business will monitor the employee's remote work;
- The procedure if technological difficulties prevent the employee from being able to work remotely;

- Any instructions issued by the company, with the participation of the workers' legal representatives, on data protection and security information as applicable to remote working;
- Intended duration of the remote working agreement.

Risk Assessment

An employer must carry out a risk assessment of the area used for remote work, which may involve the employee communicating any health and safety risks they identify or may require the employer to visit the worker's home:

> The risk assessment and the planning of the preventive activity of remote work must take into account the risks characteristic of this type of work, paying special attention to the psychosocial, ergonomic and organizational factors and the accessibility of the effective work environment. In particular, the distribution of the day, the availability times and the guarantee of breaks and disconnections during the day must be taken into account.
>
> (Official State Gazette, 2021)

Teleworker Rights to Equal Treatment, Opportunity, and Privacy

Rights of teleworkers include those of training, promotion, provision of necessary means, equipment, and tools, payment and compensation of expenses, and flexible hours.

Remote workers have the right to adequate protection in terms of safety and health at work, in accordance with the relevant law.

The employee's privacy is protected: an employer may not require applications or software to be installed of devices used by the employee to perform remote work.

Teleworkers also have the right to equal treatment, opportunities, and non-discrimination:

Remote workers must not incur any negative consequences from working from home and are ensured the same rights that they would have if working on-site. Specifically, they cannot be discriminated against with regard to working hours, training, or promotions.

The employer is required to provide the remote worker with the tools and equipment necessary to work from home:

> In accordance with the provisions of the applicable regulations, companies must take into account the particularities of remote work, especially telework, in the configuration and application of measures

against sexual harassment, harassment for reasons of sex, harassment for cause discriminatory and workplace harassment.

(Official State Gazette, 2021)

Those working remotely, particularly teleworking, have the right to digital disconnection outside of their working hours.

Portugal

In November 2021, Portugal's parliament approved new rules on remote working. Under these rules, employers could face penalties for contacting workers outside of office hours. Companies also have to help pay for expenses incurred by remote working, such as higher electricity and internet bills. The rules do not apply to companies with fewer than 10 employees (Bateman, 2021). Portugal makes it illegal for a boss to text you after work in "game changer" remote work law.

Burnout: A Global Problem

The World Health Organization (WHO) added burnout to its International Classification of Diseases in May 2019. Burnout is included in the 11th Revision of the International Classification of Diseases (ICD-11) as an occupational phenomenon. (Burnout had been included in ICD-10 in the same category as in ICD-11, but the new definition is more detailed.) It is not classified as a medical condition.

Under the Classification, burnout is described as:

Factors influencing health status or contact with health services— which includes reasons for which people contact health services but that are not classed as illnesses or health conditions.
Burn-out refers specifically to phenomena in the occupational context; it should not be applied to describe experiences in other areas of life.

(World Health Organization, 2019)

Burnout is defined in ICD-11 as follows:

Burn-out is a syndrome conceptualized as resulting from chronic workplace stress that has not been successfully managed. It is characterized by three dimensions:

- Feelings of energy depletion or exhaustion;
- Increased mental distance from one's job, or feelings of negativism or cynicism related to one's job; and
- Reduced professional efficacy.

Again, burn-out refers specifically to phenomena in the occupational context and should not be applied to describe experiences in other areas of life.

Causes of Burnout

Characteristics that contribute to burnout include:

- Workload, meaning excessive work demands or too much of the wrong kind of work;
- Control, meaning no authority to do what is needed to reach your work goals, or at a minimum you believe that you do not have the authority to do what is needed to reach those goals or do not believe that you have the support to meet those goals;
- Reward, meaning inadequate rewards in terms of money, recognition, or job satisfaction;
- Isolation from the job or the business or frequent conflict with co-workers;
- Fairness, seeing pay inequality, favoritism, or disrespect;
- Values, unethical work, or conflicting work goals.

Burnout can come from a combination of any of these. (World Health Organization, n.d.).

Burnout is a spectrum that can be measured:

> Burnout is not binary. Most believe that one has the condition or does not have it. Yet it is actually a spectrum and one that starts with seemingly harmless symptoms.
>
> (Weiss, 2020)

Belgium's Federal Public Service for Employment, Labor and Social Dialogue states:

> Burnout appears in so-called "normal" people, without mental disorder.
> Emotional exhaustion is the central dimension, leading to fatigue and eventually depression.
> The emphasis is on mental and behavioral symptoms rather than physical symptoms.
> It is a negative individual experience that influences feelings, attitudes, motivations and expectations …
> Generally speaking, burnout appears when the worker is unable to do his job as he should or as he would like to do.

This impossibility results from:

- Work constraints: an overload of work, unrealistic results object-ives, a lack of training, a lack of recognition, too great a diffe-rence between the "ideal" work for the worker (that is to say his own representations function) and concrete work;
- The workers' resources: their skills, their freedom of action, the support of colleagues, of the hierarchy, etc.

(Federal Public Service for Employment,
Labor and Social Dialogue, n.d.)

Burnout has become an unfortunate consequence of today's 'always on' world of work. The equilibrium between personal life and work life is a psychosocial hazard to which close and continual attention must be paid by organizations and employees alike—especially now.

Note

1 Codes of practice are written guidelines, agreed in a consultative process, setting out guidance and best practice for employers and employees with respect to compliance with employment legislation.

References and Further Reading

Bateman, T. (2021, November 11). Portugal makes it illegal for your boss to text you after work in "game changer" remote work law. Euronews.next. Available at www.euronews.com/next/2021/11/08/portugal-makes-it-illegal-for-your-boss-to-text-you-after-work. Accessed November 12, 2021.

Eurofound. (2021). *Right to disconnect: Exploring company practices.* Luxembourg: European Union. Available at www.eurofound.europa.eu/sites/default/files/ef_publication/field_ef_document/ef21049en.pdf. Accessed October 3, 2021.

Federal Public Service for Employment, Labor and Social Dialogue. (n.d.). Psychosocial risks at work: Definition and scope. Available at https://emploi.belgique.be/fr/themes/bien-etre-au-travail/risques-psychosociaux-au-travail/definitions-et-champ-dapplication. Accessed November 9, 2021.

Health and Safety Authority. (n.d.). Bullying at work. Available at www.hsa.ie/eng/Workplace_Health/Bullying_at_Work. Accessed September 19, 2021.

Hughes, O. (2021). Ireland gave all employees a right to disconnect, now UK workers want one, too. Available at www.techrepublic.com/article/ireland-gave-all-employees-a-right-to-disconnect-now-uk-workers-want-one-too. Accessed July 19, 2021.

Mayo Clinic. (2021). Job burnout: How to spot it and take action. Available at www.mayoclinic.org/healthy-lifestyle/adult-health/in-depth/burnout/art-20046642. Accessed October 13, 2021.

Mensah, A., & Adjei, N.K. (2020). Work–life balance and self-reported health among working adults in Europe: a gender and welfare state regime comparative analysis. *BMC Public Health*, 20, 1052. Available at https://doi.org/10.1186/s12889-020-09139-w. Accessed October 27, 2021.

Official State Gazette. (2021). *Law 10/2021 of July 9, on Remote Work*. Available at www.boe.es/eli/es/l/2021/07/09/10. Accessed October 26, 2021.

Weiss, L. (2020, October 20). Burnout from an organizational perspective. *Stanford Social Innovation Review*. Available at https://ssir.org/articles/entry/burnout_from_an_organizational_perspective#. Accessed July 19, 2021.

Williams, Z., Salter, L. & Loria, K. (2017, August 22). This is why American workers burn out faster than others. *Business Insider*. Available at www.businessinsider.com/labor-force-why-american-workers-burn-out-faster-than-others-2017-8. Accessed October 13, 2021.

Workplace Relations Commission. (2021). *Code of Practice for Employers and Employees on the Right to Disconnect*. Available at www.workplacerelations.ie/wrc/en/what_you_should_know/codes_practice/code-of-practice-for-employers-and-employees-on-the-right-to-disconnect.pdf. Accessed July 19, 2021.

World Health Organization. (2019). Burn-out an "occupational phenomenon": International Classification of Diseases. Available at www.who.int/news/item/28-05-2019-burn-out-an-occupational-phenomenon-international-classification-of-diseases. Accessed September 9, 2021.

World Health Organization. (n.d.). Mental health in the workplace. Available at www.who.int/teams/mental-health-and-substance-use/mental-health-in-the-workplace. Accessed September 9, 2021.

Chapter 9

The United Kingdom
Measures to Address Work-related Stress

Assessing Work-related Stress

Work-related stress, depression, and anxiety account for 44 percent of work-related ill-health and 54 percent of working days lost in the United Kingdom. Over 11 million work-days are lost each year because of stress at work. (Health and Safety Executive, n.d.).

Research indicates that the biggest causes of stress at work are:

- Workload (74 percent);
- Cuts in staff (53 percent);
- Changes at work (44 percent);
- Long hours (39 percent) (Asquith, 2020).

How to Resist the "Resilience" Narrative and Organize for Less Stressful Work

The U.K. Health and Safety Executive (HSE)[1] defines stress as "the adverse reaction people have to excessive pressure or other types of demand placed on them." It takes the position that work-related stress should be treated like any other workplace hazard.

Assessing Work-related Stress

The HSE states that employers have a legal duty to protect employees from stress at work by doing a risk assessment and acting on it.

A risk assessment for work-related stress includes:

- Identifying the main risk factors;
- Helping employers focus on the underlying causes and their prevention; and

DOI: 10.4324/9781003187349-11

- Providing a yardstick by which organizations can gauge their performance in tackling the key causes of stress. (Health and Safety Executive, 2021)

The HSE's suggestions for control measures that might be applied to improve the working environment include the following:

- Reduce the monotony of tasks where appropriate;
- Ensure a reasonable workload (neither too much nor too little);
- Ensure good communication and reporting of problems;
- Encourage teamwork;
- Monitor and control shiftwork or overtime working;
- Provide appropriate training.
  (Health and Safety Executive, 2020)

Under the U.K. Management of Health and Safety at Work Regulations 1999, the employer must legally carry out, at a minimum:

- Identification of what could cause injury or illness in the business (hazards);
- Determination of how likely it is that someone could be harmed and how seriously (the risk);
- Action to eliminate the hazard, or if this is not possible, control the risk.

Health and Safety Executive Management Standards

The U.K. Health and Safety Executive (HSE) Management Standards provide a systematic approach to implementing an organizational procedure for managing work-related stress.

The HSE introduced the Management Standards in 2004 to help employers to identify and manage the causes of work-related stress and to implement solutions to manage relevant risks posed by stress at work.

The Management Standards are not legally enforceable, but offer a guidance-based approach to work-related stress, taking into account relevant requirements of the Health and Safety at Work Act 1974 and the Management of Health and Safety at Work Regulations 1999. These laws require that employers carry out an assessment of significant health and safety risks, including the risk of stress-related ill-health arising from work activities, and implement measures to control these risks.

The Management Standards help to identify and manage six areas of work—demands, control, support, relationships, role, and change—that can lead to stress if not properly managed. These areas often combine, overlap, or interact.

Implementing the Management Standards Approach

Appropriate resources, support, and infrastructure must be in place in an organization to effectively implement the Management Standards approach. Employees and the employer should work together.

The HSE suggests that the following players be included in preparing the organization for the Management Standards approach:

- Senior management and line managers;
- Health and safety managers;
- Trade union health and safety representatives or employee representatives;
- Human resources and occupational health representatives.

The first step for an organisation implementing the Management Standards approach is to set up a working group to oversee the stress risk assessment process. This can be the existing safety committee or a group set up specifically for this purpose. There should be union involvement, but it is also important that, where available, HR, health and safety and occupational health specialists are on the group. Also remember that the approach is organisational, covering all levels of staff within the organisation … Where possible, this group should include a senior manager (at Director or Board level) to show commitment and to confirm resources for the project.
(Health and Safety Executive, 2009, pp. 8–9)

The second step is the risk assessment process: if work causes stress, then all the risks—not just the psychological risks—must be assessed on the basis of the following five steps:

1. Identify the risk factors.
2. Who can be harmed and how?
3. Evaluate the risks.
4. Record the findings.
5. Monitor and review the effectiveness of any control measures to ensure they have been implemented properly and are working effectively, and to establish whether there have been any new issues.

The HSE states that the Management Standards

represent a set of conditions that, if present:

- Demonstrate good practice through a step-by-step risk assessment approach

- Allow assessment of the current situation using pre-existing data, surveys and other techniques
- Promote active discussion and working in partnership with employees and their representatives, to help decide on practical improvements that can be made
- Require staff and employer to work together
- Help simplify risk assessment for work-related stress by identifying the main risk factors
- Help employers focus on the underlying causes and their prevention
- Provide a yardstick by which organisations can gauge their performance in tackling the key causes of stress.

(Health and Safety Executive, 2019)

Management Standard Specifics

The full text of the Management Standards is included below.

Demands—includes issues such as workload, work patterns, and the work environment

- Employees indicate that they are able to cope with the demands of their jobs; and
- Systems are in place locally to respond to any individual concerns.

What should be happening:

- The organisation provides employees with adequate and achievable demands in relation to the agreed hours of work;
- People's skills and abilities are matched to the job demands;
- Jobs are designed to be within the capabilities of employees;
- Employees' concerns about their work environment are addressed.

Under each area there are "states to be achieved," which organisations should work towards.

Control—how much say a person has in the way they do their work

The Standard is that:

- Employees indicate that they are able to have a say about the way they do their work; and
- Systems are in place locally to respond to any individual concerns.

What should be happening/states to be achieved:

- Where possible, employees have control over their pace of work;
- Employees are encouraged to use their skills and initiative to do their work;
- Where possible, employees are encouraged to develop new skills to help them undertake new and challenging pieces of work;
- The organisation encourages employees to develop their skills;
- Employees have a say over when breaks can be taken; and

Employees are consulted over their work patterns.

Support—includes the encouragement, sponsorship and resources provided by the organisation, line management, and colleagues.

The Standard is that:

- Employees indicate that they receive adequate information and support from their colleagues and superiors; and
- Systems are in place locally to respond to any individual concerns.

What should be happening/States to be achieved:

- The organisation has policies and procedures to adequately support employees;
- Systems are in place to enable and encourage managers to support their staff;
- Systems are in place to enable and encourage employees to support their colleagues;
- Employees know what support is available and how and when to access it;
- Employees know how to access the required resources to do their job; and
- Employees receive regular and constructive feedback.

Relationships—includes promoting positive working to avoid conflict and dealing with unacceptable behaviour

The Standard is that:

- Employees indicate that they are not subjected to unacceptable behaviours, e.g., bullying at work; and
- Systems are in place locally to respond to any individual concerns.

What should be happening/states to be achieved:

- The organisation promotes positive behaviours at work to avoid conflict and ensure fairness;
- Employees share information relevant to their work;
- The organisation has agreed policies and procedures to prevent or resolve unacceptable behaviour;
- Systems are in place to enable and encourage managers to deal with unacceptable behaviour; and
- Systems are in place to enable and encourage employees to report unacceptable behaviour.

Role—whether people understand their role within the organisation and whether the organisation ensures that they do not have conflicting roles
   The Standard is that:

- Employees indicate that they understand their role and responsibilities; and
- Systems are in place locally to respond to any individual concerns.

What should be happening/states to be achieved:

- The organisation ensures that, as far as possible, the different requirements it places upon employees are compatible;
- The organisation provides information to enable employees to understand their role and responsibilities;
- The organisation ensures that, as far as possible, the requirements it places upon employees are clear; and
- Systems are in place to enable employees to raise concerns about any uncertainties or conflicts they have in their role and responsibilities.

Change—how organisational change (large or small) is managed and communicated in the organization
   The Standard is that:

- Employees indicate that the organisation engages them frequently when undergoing an organisational change; and
- Systems are in place locally to respond to any individual concerns.

What should be happening/states to be achieved:

- The organisation provides employees with timely information to enable them to understand the reasons for proposed changes;
- The organisation ensures adequate employee consultation on changes and provides opportunities for employees to influence proposals;
- Employees are aware of the probable impact of any changes to their jobs. If necessary, employees are given training to support any changes in their jobs;
- Employees are aware of timetables for changes; and
- Employees have access to relevant support during changes.

Tools and Resources

The HSE has issued a number of tools associated with the Management Standards process, including *How to Tackle Work-related Stress: A Guide for Employers on Making the Management Standards Work* (2019), a workbook that helps employers to prepare for and conduct an appropriate risk assessment and that offers measures to take based on the results.

The guide states:

> The Management Standards approach requires managers, employees and their representatives to work together to improve certain areas of work, described in the Standards, which will have a positive effect on employee wellbeing. The approach is aimed at the organisation rather than individuals, so that a larger number of employees can benefit from any actions taken.
>
> (HSE, 2009, p 2)

The HSE has also published the Management Standards Indicator Tool, a questionnaire with 35 questions for an organization to determine present working conditions and monitor future ones. The tool is available at www.hse.gov.uk/stress/assets/docs/indicatortool.pdf. (More tools and resources are contained in the Appendix.)

Unions and Tackling Workplace Stress Using the HSE Management Standards

The U.K. Trades Union Congress (TUC), comprising 5.5 million working people and 48 member unions, worked with the HSE to publish guidance for union health and safety representatives. The guide is designed to help union safety representatives to encourage their employer to work with them to implement the HSE Management Standards approach to managing work-related stress. It includes a background to the problem of stress, outlines what the Management Standards are, and explains what an employer can do and where to go for additional information:

> Unions and employers working together to invest in health and safety can result in a vast improvement in other aspects of industrial relations and a working environment in which work-related stress is managed properly.
>
> (TUC, 2017)

A Word About Loneliness

The estimated cost of loneliness to UK employers is £2.5 billion every year, primarily due to increased staff turnover (64%, £1.62 billion) and lower wellbeing and productivity (26%, £665 million)

In May 2021, the U.K.'s Department for Digital, Culture, Media and Sport published guidance titled 'Employers and loneliness', to address what organizations can do to tackle loneliness among their workers. The guidance is based on consultation with businesses and employers who recognize loneliness in the workplace and support employees' social wellbeing.

The guidance states:

> Having good quality meaningful connections is associated with better outcomes in terms of quality of work, higher wellbeing and greater engagement in work. Across work roles, a lack of social connection and loneliness can lead to less commitment and productivity and greater absenteeism and staff turnover, and employees who feel lonely appear less approachable to their colleagues.
>
> (Department for Digital, Culture, Media and Sport, 2021)

Five key themes were identified to tackle loneliness at work:

- *Culture and infrastructure:* identifying what really matters to employees and aligning with corporate values and embedding loneliness into other wellbeing and welfare activities.
- *Management:* the kinds of support and guidance which can help managers to identify and help the people working for them who are experiencing loneliness and the training that managers might need.
- *People and networks:* how people have used networks to tackle loneliness including whilst working remotely.

- *Work and workplace design:* How employers have tackled a dispersed workforce, and the tools and systems that can promote visibility and connections.
- *Wider role in the community:* How some employers have sought to tackle loneliness beyond our immediate workforce.

The guidance contains examples of ways to alleviate loneliness (Department for Digital, Culture, Media and Sport, 2021).

Note

1 HSE's work covers a varied range of activities such as shaping and reviewing regulations, producing research and statistics, and enforcing the law.

References and Further Reading

Asquith, S. (2020). How to resist the "resilience" narrative—and organise for less stressful work. TUC blog. Available at www.tuc.org.uk/blogs/how-resist-resilie nce-narrative-and-organise-less-stressful-work. Accessed September 18, 2021.

Department for Digital, Culture, Media & Sport and Office for Civil Society. (2018). UK Government's work on tackling loneliness. Available at www. gov.uk/government/collections/governments-work-on-tackling-loneliness. Accessed October 4, 2021.

Department for Digital, Culture, Media & Sport. (2021). *Emerging together: The Tackling Loneliness Network action plan.* Available at www.gov.uk/governm ent/publications/emerging-together-the-tackling-loneliness-network-action-plan. Accessed July 19, 2021.

Government Equalities Office. (2021). Consultation on sexual harassment in the workplace: Government response. Available at www.gov.uk/government/ consultations/consultation-on-sexual-harassment-in-the-workplace/outcome/ consultation-on-sexual-harassment-in-the-workplace-government-response. Accessed August 3, 2021.

Health and Safety Executive. (2009). *How to tackle work-related stress: A guide for employers on making the Management Standards work.* Available at www. hse.gov.uk/pubns/indg430.pdf. Accessed September 24, 2021.

Health and Safety Executive. (2019). What are the Management Standards? Available at www.hse.gov.uk/stress/standards/index.htm. Accessed October 23, 2021.

Health and Safety Executive. (n.d.). Managing risks and risk assessment at work. Available at www.hse.gov.uk/simple-health-safety/risk/risk-assessment-templ ate-and-examples.htm. Accessed November 10, 2021.

Health and Safety Executive. (2009). *Tackling work-related stress using the Management Standards approach: A step-by-step workbook.* Available at www.hse.gov.uk/pubns/indg430.pdf. Accessed September 19, 2021.

Health and Safety Executive. (2020). What are psychosocial risk factors? What can I do to reduce the risks of psychosocial factors? Available at www.hse.gov. uk/msd/mac/psychosocial.htm. Accessed September 19, 2021.

Health and Safety Executive. (2020). Work-related stress, anxiety or depression statistics in Great Britain. Available at www.hse.gov.uk/statistics/causdis/stress.pdf. Accessed September 18, 2021.

Health and Safety Executive. (2021). Do I have to follow the Management Standards approach? Available at www.hse.gov.uk/stress/standards/doi.htm. Accessed November 9, 2021.

Health and Safety Executive. (n.d.). Stress risk assessment. Available at www.hse.gov.uk/stress/risk-assessment.htm. Accessed November 9, 2021.

Health and Safety Executive. (n.d.). Work-related stress. Available at www.hse.gov.uk/stress. Accessed November 9, 2021.

Legislation.gov.UK. (1974). *UK Health and Safety at Work Act.* Available at www.legislation.gov.uk/ukpga/1974/37. Accessed October 25, 2021.

Legislation.gov.UK. (1999). The Management of Health and Safety at Work Regulations, No. 3242/1999. Available at www.legislation.gov.uk/uksi/1999/3242/contents/made. Accessed October 25, 2021.

Milczarek, M. & Irastorza, X. (2012). *Drivers and barriers for psychosocial risk management: An analysis of the findings of the European Survey of Enterprises on New and Emerging Risks.* Brussels: European Agency for Safety and Health at Work. Available at: www.researchgate.net/publication/301698437_Drivers_and_barriers_for_psychosocial_risk_management_an_analysis_of_the_findings_of_the_European_Survey_of_Enterprises_on_New_and_Emerging_Risks. Accessed October 21, 2021.

TUC-HSE. (2017). Tackling workplace stress using the HSE Stress Management Standards. Available at www.tuc.org.uk/sites/default/files/tacking-workplace-stress-guide.pdf. Accessed October 25, 2021.

Chapter 10

Mexico Mandates Protection from Workplace Psychosocial Risks

Mexico has the highest rate of workplace stress in the world. According to the World Health Organization (WHO), Mexico has a 75 percent prevalence of stress in its workforce, which places it on the first rung above the world's leading economies. The Organization for Economic Cooperation and Development (OECD) has estimated that 43 percent of Mexico's workers suffer from burnout. The OECD also found that Mexicans work an average of 2,255 hours a year—492 more than workers in other countries.

Work-related anxiety and depression cost Mexico more than US$834 million in productivity per year and work-related stress reduces gross domestic product by between 0.5 and 3.5 percent, according to some calculations.

Mexico's Nom-035 on Psychosocial Risks

Mexico has enacted a comprehensive law aimed at preventing mental health issues and psychological risk factors in the workplace. NOM-035-STPS-2018 charges all employers with the obligation to identify, analyze, and prevent work-related psychological risks, which are described as those that may trigger anxiety, sleep, stress, and adaptation disorders.

Mexico issued NOM-035-STPS-2018 Psychological Risk Factors at work – Identification, Analysis and Prevention (NOM-035), which took full effect on October 23, 2019. It establishes the elements required to identify, analyze, and prevent job-related psychosocial risks that may harm employees' physical, social, and mental health.

NOM-035 is intended to reduce occupational burnout caused by stress and violence in the workplace as well as to promote a favorable organizational environment in the workplace.

DOI: 10.4324/9781003187349-12

NOM-035 recognizes that three major risk factors can trigger various types of illnesses in employees in Mexico:

- Work-related stress;
- Work-related violence; and
- A general lack of high-quality sleep.

If not addressed in their early stages, these issues can lead to a wide range of additional problems, including depression, anxiety, and alcoholism. From a workplace perspective, they can also lead to high levels of absenteeism, employee disengagement, a high turnover rate, and a significant decline in productivity and profitability.

Nom-035 states:

> Stress is commonly defined as a perceived imbalance between the demands made on people and their resources or ability to cope with those demands. Although the experience of stress might appear primarily psychological, stress also affects physical health. The symptoms of stress can result in increased absenteeism, high turnover, disciplinary problems, violence and psychological harassment, reduced productivity, as well as reduced attention, mistakes and accidents. Factors, both inside and outside the workplace, can influence health. Poorly managed work features, such as constant high job demands, tight deadlines, harassment, and unsupportive managerial style, are likely to provoke the feeling of stress in workers. Legally, all employers have a general duty to ensure the health and safety of workers in every aspect of their work.
>
> (Mexlaws.com, 2018)

Nom-035 defines psychosocial risk factors as

> those that can cause anxiety disorders, a non-organic sleep-wake cycle and severe stress and adaptation derived from the nature of the functions of the job position in the workplace, the type of work shift and the exposure to severe traumatic events or acts of labor violence to the worker, for the work carried out.

They include the following:

- Dangerous and unsafe conditions in the work environment;
- Workloads when they exceed the capacity of the worker;
- The lack of control over work (possibility of influencing the organization and carrying out of the work when the process allows it);

- Working days in excess of those provided for in the Federal Labor Law;
- Rotation of shifts that include a night shift and a night shift without recovery and rest periods;
- Interference in the work-family relationship; and
- Negative leadership and negative relationships at work.

(Mexlaws.com, 2018)

Applicability and Employer Requirements

NOM-035 is applicable in all workplaces, but with different obligations depending on the number of employees in the workplace: obligations are grouped into 15 workers; 16–50 workers; and more than 50 workers. Workplaces of up to 15 workers are exempt from the law.

The employer is required to implement measures to identify, analyze, prevent, and control work-related psychosocial factors that could harm the physical and mental health of employees. Measures to do this include:

- Establishing in-depth workplace psychosocial risk prevention policies, actions, and programs;
- Disseminating the policy and measures adopted to reduce psychosocial risks to employees;
- Conducting training for certain employees;
- Performing identification and analysis of psychosocial risk factors; and
- Evaluating the organizational environment.

The employer's additional obligations under the rule include the following responsibilities:

- Identify psychosocial risk factors and evaluate the organizational environment (for workplaces with over 50 employees);
- Use questionnaires to identify psychosocial risk factors (for workplaces with 16–50 employees);
- Identify the employees subject to psychosocial damages while working or derived from their work;
- Provide a registry where employees can learn about psychosocial risk factors identified in the workplace and corrective actions taken;
- Implement a confidential complaint system so employees can inform the employer about psychosocial risk factors;
- Take action to prevent psychosocial risk factors and corrective measures if psychosocial damage occurs.

NOM-035 also requires the employer to:

- Communicate, implement, and keep job health and safety protocols to prevent harassment and violence in the job;
- Procure a positive organizational environment;
- Identify and treat employees who are exposed to severe trauma;
- Perform medical examinations for those employees exposed to psychosocial risks and job-related violence.

Psychosocial Risk-prevention Policy

NOM-035 calls for the employer to have a psychosocial risk prevention policy, defined as a statement of principles and commitments that establishes the pattern to prevent psychosocial risk factors and workplace violence, and to promote a favorable organizational environment in order to develop a culture in which decent work is sought, and the continuous improvement of working conditions. (See Reference Guide IV for an example of a psychosocial risk-prevention policy.)

Written policies for all three tiers of the workplace must include the following factors:

- The prevention of psychosocial risk factors;
- The prevention of workplace violence;
- The promotion of a favorable organizational environment;
- Measures to prevent and control psychosocial risk factors;
- Addressing practices that are contrary to the favorable organizational environment and acts of workplace violence.

In workplaces with 16–50 employees and those with more than 50, the employer must also identify workers who were subject to severe traumatic events during or due to work, and channel them to the social or private security institution for their attention, or to the doctor at the workplace or the company.

In addition, employers in workplaces with over 50 employees must perform medical examinations and psychological evaluations to workers exposed to workplace violence and/or psychosocial risk factors.

In all workplaces with 15 or more employees, the employer must provide information to workers on the following:

- The policy of prevention of psychosocial risks;
- The measures adopted to combat the practices opposed to the favorable organizational environment and Acts of labor violence;
- The measures and preventive actions for psychosocial risk factors;

- Mechanisms for filing complaints and to report acts of violence;
- The results of the identification and analysis of psychosocial risk factors;
- Possible alterations to health due to exposure to psychosocial risk factors.

(Mexlaws.com, 2018)

Identification and Analysis of Psychosocial Risk Factors

Workplaces that have more than 50 workers must carry out the identification and analysis of the psychosocial risk factors and the evaluation of the organizational environment; this can be done with a representative sampling.

The identification and analysis of psychosocial risk factors must include the following:

- Conditions in the work environment;
- Workload;
- Lack of control over the work;
- Workdays and rotation of shifts that exceed what is established in the Federal Labor Law;
- Interference in the work–family relationship;
- Negative leadership and negative relationships at work;
- Workplace violence, pursuant to sexual harassment, psychological harassment, or mistreatment.

The evaluation of the favorable organizational environment includes:

- The sense of belonging of the workers to the company;
- Training for the proper performance of the tasks entrusted;
- The precise definition of responsibilities for workers;
- Proactive participation and communication between the employer, its representatives and the workers;
- Adequate distribution of workloads, with regular working hours;
- The evaluation and recognition of performance.

Workplaces may use the application of questionnaires for the evaluation. The questionnaires must include the following:

- The identification and analysis of psychosocial risk factors and the evaluation of the organizational environment;
- The results of the identification and analysis of the psychosocial risk factors and the evaluation of the organizational environment must be contained in a report;

- The result of the identification and analysis of the psychosocial risk factors and the evaluation of the organizational environment should be available for consultation of the workers;
- The identification and analysis of psychosocial risk factors and the evaluation of the organizational environment should be carried out at least every two years.

(Mexlaws.com, 2018)

Nom-035's Reference Guides

Nom-035 includes five reference guides at the end of the legislation.

- *Reference Guide I:* sample questionnaire to identify workers who have been subjected to severe traumatic events. The content of this guide is a complement for the better understanding of this Standard and is not mandatory. An example of a questionnaire is presented that allows the identification of workers who have been subjected to severe traumatic events and require clinical evaluation.
- *Reference Guide II:* identification and analysis of psychosocial risk factors. May be carried out by applying this questionnaire; it can be used by workplaces with up to 50 workers.
- *Reference Guide III:* identification and analysis of psychosocial risk factors and evaluation of the organizational environment in the work centers. Non-mandatory and can be used by those work centers with more than 50 workers.
- *Reference Guide IV:* example of a policy for the prevention of psychosocial risks.
- *Reference Guide V:* worker data.

Lack of Sleep as a Risk Factor

Mexico's Nom-035 identifies a general lack of high-quality sleep as one of the three risk factors that can trigger various types of employee illnesses.

Fatigue in the workplace is an important health and safety concern: when it comes to sleep's role in the workplace, safety, productivity, performance, health, and morale may all be impacted.

Highly fatigued workers are 70 percent more likely to be involved in accidents. The National Sleep Foundation states:

> There is overwhelming evidence demonstrating that sleep deprivation leads to workplace accidents. Overly sleepy employees are 70% more likely to be involved in workplace accidents than colleagues who are not sleep-deprived.

(Foley, 2021)

Workplace catastrophes due to fatigue include:

- The Union Carbide chemical plant in Bhopal;
- The Chernobyl nuclear reactor disaster;
- Three Mile Island; and
- Exxon-Valdez.

A lack of sufficient sleep can cause:

- Workplace accidents;
- Lost productivity;
- Absenteeism;
- Presenteeism;
- Impaired reaction time and judgment;
- Short-term memory and information-processing problems;
- Decreased performance and motivation;
- More difficulty with concentration and handling stress.

Why Sleep Matters: The Economic Costs of Insufficient Sleep (Hafner et al., 2016) quantifies the economic losses due to lack of sleep among workers in five different countries: the United States, the United Kingdom, Canada, Germany, and Japan. Marco Hafner, a research leader at RAND Europe and the study's main author, states:

> Our study shows that the effects from a lack of sleep are massive. Sleep deprivation not only influences an individual's health and well-being but has a significant impact on a nation's economy, with lower productivity levels and a higher mortality risk among workers ... Improving individual sleep habits and duration has huge implications, with our research showing that simple changes can make a big difference.
>
> (Hafner et al., 2016)

Statistics for various countries show the impact of insufficient sleep:

- The United States sustained the highest economic losses (up to $411 billion a year, which is 2.28 percent of its GDP) due to the size of its economy, with the most working days (1.2 million) lost due to sleep deprivation among its workforce.
- Japan followed (up to $138 billion a year, which is 2.92 percent of its GDP), or approximately 600,000 working days lost.
- Germany was next (up to $60 billion, or 1.56 percent of its GDP) and just over 200,000 working days lost.

- The United Kingdom followed (up to $50 billion, 1.86 percent of its GDP). Sleep deprivation leads to the United Kingdom losing around 200,000 working days a year.
- Canada was the nation with the best sleep outcomes and the lowest financial losses due to lack of sleep (up to $21.4 billion, which is 1.35 percent of its GDP) and just under 80,000 working days lost).

To improve sleep outcomes, employers should recognize the importance of sleep and the employer's role in its promotion; design and build brighter workspaces; combat workplace psychosocial risks; and discourage the extended use of electronic devices.

Social and Behavioral Costs of Sleeplessness to the Workplace

Poor sleep negatively impacts workplace relationships and social behavior.

Getting sufficient sleep increases job satisfaction, according to research, while also reducing job-related stress. One large study showed sleep-deprived workers perceived their jobs to be more demanding, felt that had less control over their work, and also felt their workplaces were less socially supportive. These employees also had higher stress levels, which in turn were linked to worse sleep at a two-year follow-up.

Studies show that poor sleep is linked to deviant behavior in the workplace, behavior that ranges from avoiding work and leaving early or arriving late, to rudeness, theft, vandalism, and violence.

The difference between sleep amounts for deviant and non-deviant behaviors is strikingly narrow. Researchers found that people who slept fewer than six hours nightly were more likely to demonstrate deviant and unethical behaviors the next day, compared with people who slept more than six hours (Hafner et al., 2016).

References and Further Reading

Breus, M. (2016, March 15). The social and behavioral costs of sleeplessness to the workplace. *Huffington Post*. Available at www.huffingtonpost.com/dr-michael-j-breus/the-social-and-behavioral-costs-of-sleeplessness-to-the-work place_b_9443162.html. Accessed July 19, 2021.

Clarke, R. (2016, November 30). Lack of sleep costing UK economy up to £40 billion a year. *HR Review*. Available at www.hrreview.co.uk/hr-news/lack-sleep-costing-uk-economy-40-billion-year/102670. Accessed September 23, 2021.

Foley, L. (2021, February 12). Excessive sleepiness and workplace accidents. Sleep Foundation Available at www.sleepfoundation.org/excessive-sleepiness/workplace-accidents. Accessed July 19, 2021.

Hafner, M., Stepanek, M., Taylor, J., Troxel, W. M. & Van Stolk, C. (2016, November 29). Why sleep matters: Quantifying the economic costs of

insufficient sleep. Rand. Available at www.rand.org/randeurope/research/proje
cts/the-value-of-the-sleep-economy.html. Accessed July 19, 2021.

Lockton. (2019, July 15). Mexico takes action on work-related psychosocial
risks. Available at www.locktoninternational.com/gb/articles/mexico-takes-act
ion-work-related-psychosocial-risks. Accessed September 23, 2021.

Maldonado, A. (2019, May 21). Work stress and why now the STPS rules for
companies to attend to it. *Forbes*. Available at www.forbes.com.mx/estres-labo
ral-y-porque-es-normativo-atenderlo. Accessed September 23, 2021.

Mexico News Daily. (2019, October 11). Mexico no. 1 country in the world for
workplace stress. Available at https://mexiconewsdaily.com/news/mexico-no-
1-country-in-the-world-for-workplace-stress. Accessed September 23, 2021.

Mexlaws.com. (2018, October 23). Mexican Laws in English, NOM-035-STPS-
2018, Occupational psychosocial risk factors—identification, analysis and
prevention. Available at www.mexlaws.com/STPS/NOM-035-STPS-2018-info
rmation.htm. Accessed September 23, 2021.

SEGOB, Diario Oficial de la Federacion. (2018, October 23). Official Mexican
NORMA NOM-035-STPS-2018: Psychosocial risk factors at work-
Identification, analysis and prevention. Available at https://dof.gob.mx/
nota_detalle.php?codigo=5541828&fecha=23%2F10%2F2018. Accessed
August 4, 2021.

Chapter 11

Canada

National Standard for Psychological Health and Safety in the Workplace

> Not addressing psychological health and safety in the workplace is a significant cost to the Canadian economy. Mental health problems and mental illnesses account for approximately 30% of short- and long-term disability claims. And they are rated one of the top causes of disability claims by over 80% of Canadian employers. Mental health conditions are the leading cause of disability, absence, and presenteeism, with an economic burden estimated at 51 billion dollars per year in Canada, 20 billion [dollars] of which is from direct workplace losses.
>
> (Mental Health Commission of Canada, 2014)

The National Standard of Canada for Psychological Health and Safety in the Workplace

The National Standard of Canada for Psychological Health and Safety in the Workplace was the first of its kind in the world.

CAN/CSA-Z1003-13/BNQ 9700-803/2013 – National Standard of Canada, Psychological Health and Safety in the Workplace – Prevention, Promotion, and Guidance to Staged Implementation CAN/CSA-Z1003-13/BNQ 9700-803/2013 (Mental Health Commission of Canada, 2013) was launched in January 2013 and reaffirmed in 2018. It offers a framework to prevent psychological injury, and is intended to guide organizations in promoting mental health and preventing psychological harm at work though a comprehensive set of voluntary guidelines, tools, and resources to implement its provisions, promote mental health, and prevent psychological harm at work.

The following are some highlights of the Standard:

- Includes information on the identification of psychological hazards in the workplace; the assessment and control of risks that cannot be

DOI: 10.4324/9781003187349-13

eliminated; implementation practices that support and promote psychological health and safety in the workplace; and systems for review and measurement of the approach;

- Voluntary, free, and offers scenarios for all sizes of organization and acts as an audit tool;
- Implemented successfully by a number of companies including a large healthcare company and Bell Canada (see below on standard-related statistics and case studies);
- Provides a comprehensive framework to help organizations of all types guide their current and future efforts in a way that provides the best return on investment. It also allows employees to seek help if needed.

When implementing the Standard, needs specific to the organization should be taken into account and departments should work together rather than implementing it separately. Adopting the Standard can help organizations with productivity, financial performance, risk management, organizational recruitment, and employee retention, as well as culture change.

The Standard has a number of guiding principles:

- Legal requirements associated with psychologically healthy and safe workplaces applicable to the organization will be identified and complied with as a minimum standard of practice;
- Psychological health and safety are a shared responsibility among all workplace stakeholders and commensurate with the authority of the stakeholder;
- The workplace is based on mutually respectful relationships among the organization, its management, its workers, and worker representatives, which includes maintaining the confidentiality of sensitive information;
- Individuals have a responsibility towards their own health and behaviour;
- A demonstrated and visible commitment by senior management for the development and sustainability of a psychologically healthy and safe workplace;
- Active participation with all workplace stakeholders;
- Organizational decision making incorporates psychological health and safety in the processes; and
- A primary focus on psychological health, safety, awareness, and promotion as well as the development of knowledge and skills for those persons managing work arrangements, organization, processes, and/or people.

- Activities associated with this Standard, specifically related to planning, data collection, and evaluation requirements, are to be conducted in a psychologically safe, confidential, and ethical manner.

(CSA Group, 2013)

The Psychological Health and Safety Management System (PHSMS)

The Standard requires that an organization establish, document, implement, and maintain a psychological health and safety management system (PHSMS) in the workplace and continually improve its effectiveness. The PHSMS should be integrated into, or compatible with, governance practices and other systems in the organization.

(CSA Group, 2013. Clause 4.2)

Adopting a PHSMS isn't about assessing a worker's mental health. It is about considering the impact of workplace processes, policies, and interactions on the psychological health and safety of all workers.

(Collins, 2014, p. 11)

An effective organizational support system for a PHSMS has three integral elements: strong organizational Commitment and Leadership; active Employee Engagement and Participation; and supportive and effective Policies and Procedures.

(Collins, 2014, pp. 32–33)

The PHSMS covers the following five areas:

- Policy, leadership, participation;
- Planning;
- Implementation and operation;
- Evaluation and corrective action;
- Management review.

Responsibilities and authorities related to the PHSMS must be defined and communicated throughout the organization. The organization must encourage worker/worker representative participation by taking the following measures:

- Providing time and resources to participate in the PHSMS program;
- Identifying and removing barriers to participation;
- Involving and training in relevant aspects of the PHSMS.

The organization must ensure participation through the following steps:

- Engaging stakeholders in regular dialogue;
- Engaging workers/worker representatives in policy development, data generation, and planning;
- Engaging the OHS committee/worker representatives in defining their involvement in the PHSMS;
- Respecting the confidentiality of persons, including the removal of identifying material on relevant documents;
- Considering the development of a specific PHSMS Committee;
- Considering the unique needs of a diverse population and soliciting input when these needs are relevant to achieving the goals of the Standard.

Planning for Management of Psychological Health and Safety

The Standard states that planning allows an organization to identify and prioritize work-related psychological health and safety in terms of hazards, risks, management system gaps, and opportunities for improvement.

The planning process includes "developing a collective vision of a psychologically healthy workplace, specific goals for reaching the vision, and a plan for ongoing process monitoring for continual improvement" (CSA, 2013, Clause 4.3.2).

The organization should start by reviewing its approach to, and its policy and processes for, managing and promoting psychological health and safety, or if these do not exist, establishing a system.

Planning involves identification, assessment of psychosocial risk factors, control of hazards, and data collection. Factors to assess should include, but are not limited to:

- Psychological support;
- Organizational culture;
- Clear leadership and expectations;
- Civility and respect;
- Psychological job demands;
- Growth and development;
- Recognition and reward;
- Involvement and influence;
- Workload management;
- Engagement;
- Work–life balance;
- Psychological protection from violence, bullying, and harassment;

- Protection of physical safety;
- Other chronic stressors as identified by workers.

The Standard also provides in-depth information on identification, assessment, and control, in accordance with the traditional hierarchy of risk control, and calls upon the organization to maintain a risk mitigation process.

Measuring Progress and Managing Change

Measuring Progress

Requirements for a documented and systematic approach to develop and sustain a psychologically healthy and safe workplace should address psychological health and safety aspects within the control, responsibility, or influence of the workplace that can impact the workforce.

The Standard states that objectives and targets should be measurable and take account of the following:

- Consistency with the psychological health and safety policy and commitment to the PHSMS;
- Compliance with any legal or other requirements;
- Determination after consultation with workers and with consideration of the organization's operational and business requirements;
- Being based on past reviews of identification and assessment of psychological workplace factors and management system deficiencies.

The organization should establish and maintain a plan for achieving its objectives and targets, which includes designating responsibility for achieving these objectives and targets, and identification of the means and timeframe within which the objectives and targets are to be achieved.

Managing Change

The organization should establish, implement, and maintain a system to manage changes that can affect psychological health and safety. These might include:

- Significant changes to work procedures, equipment, organizational structure, staffing, products, services, or suppliers;
- Changes to psychological health and safety strategies and practices;
- Changes to work arrangements, including modified work arrangements.

The system should include communication between stakeholders about changes, information and training sessions for workers and worker representatives, and any necessary support for the worker.

The organization should provide and sustain necessary infrastructure and resources to achieve conformity with the Standard:

- Parties in the workplace should possess sufficient authority and resources to fulfill their duties related to the Standard; and
- Persons with roles specified in the Standard should possess the knowledge, skills, and abilities to carry out their roles.

Note that internal or external resources may be looked to in order to provide substantial expertise, programs, or assistance in implementing psychological health and safety programs in the workplace.

The Standard also contains sections on implementation (Clause 4.4), evaluation and corrective action (Clause 4.5), and management review (Clause 5).

Standard-related Statistics and Case Studies
Implementing the Standard

The Standard has been implemented by organizations of all sizes and in all sectors. The statistics below show the positive impact on organizations of implementing the Standard compared with those that have not.

- Ten percent of employees who work for an organization that is implementing the Standard describe a workplace that has serious or significant concerns, while 37 percent of those who work for an organization without the Standard describe a concerning workplace.
- Fifty-six percent of those whose organization is implementing the Standard describe the psychological environment as a relative strength, compared with just 31 percent of those whose organization has not implemented the Standard.
- Among organizations implementing the Standard, 5 percent of employees say their workplace is psychologically unhealthy, compared with 13 percent in organizations that are not implementing the Standard, who say their workplace is psychologically unhealthy or unsafe.
- At organizations that are implementing the Standard, employees who are experiencing or have experienced depression are spending less time (7.4 days per year) away from work compared with those whose organization is not implementing the Standard (12.5 days) (Ipsos Reid, 2017).

Mental Health Commission of Canada, Case Study Research Project

The Mental Health Commission of Canada (MHCC) launched a three-year national Case Study Research Project (CSRP) in 2014 to better understand how workplaces of all sizes and sectors across Canada are implementing the National Standard of Canada for Psychological Health and Safety in the Workplace.

The *Case Study Research Project Final Report* (Mental Health Commission oof Canada, 2017) is a summary of encouraging practices and lessons learned from 40 participating organizations. It synthesizes their experiences and discoveries to support other Canadian employers in taking steps to promote employee psychological health and prevent psychological harm in their own workplaces.

Tools and Resources for Implementing the Standard

The Mental Health Commission of Canada (MHCC) has developed a variety of resources to help organizations create more mentally healthy work environments and support implementation of the Standard.

Assembling the Pieces

The MHCC offers a free online toolkit designed to support organizations working to implement the Standard; it is recommended for employers, senior leaders, human resource managers, and occupational health and safety professionals.

Guarding Minds@Work is a comprehensive set of resources designed to assess and address workplace psychological health and safety. It is designed to align with the Standard and available to employers free of charge.

Guarding Minds helps to assess organizations against the National Standard of Canada on psychological health and safety in the workplace through its provision of tools such as an organizational review process, and action planning tools and worksheets. The tools are intended to be administered by an employee of the organization, but the organization may also choose to hire a workplace psychological health and safety consultant to administer it.

Guarding Minds includes the following resources:

- Assessment tools, including an organizational review process for leadership, an online employee survey and a shorter stress scan;
- A comprehensive Guarding Minds@Work report to identify areas for improvement;

- Action planning process and worksheets;
- An evaluation process to measure progress and outcomes.

The sample audit tool is an annex of the Standard and may be used by an organization to conduct internal audits. The audit tool is intended as a gap analysis tool that will provide the organization with a baseline measurement of current status and reveal what areas that require further work to meet the requirements of the Standard. It may be modified to suit the size, nature, and complexity of the organization.

Union and Management Cooperation: Workplace Strategies for Mental Health

The National Standard of Canada for Psychological Health and Safety in the Workplace provides a framework that can be used to help employers and unions work together to support a psychologically healthy and safe workplace:

> While there may be union representatives who do not use psychologically safe approaches in the workplaces, much like psychologically unsafe employers, this is changing.
>
> (Workplace Strategies for Mental Health, n.d.)

Employers can benefit from the union representative's knowledge and ability to support planning, implementation, and the ongoing sustainability of a psychologically healthy and safe workplace in ways including the following:

- Promoting social support: Encourage a culture of respect and inclusion where workers value one another;
- Providing information and resources: Educate members on both rights and responsibilities associated with the accommodation process. Help workers who may be experiencing mental health concerns access resources and expertise available in the organization and community;
- Engaging workers in the discussion: Help workers be active in identifying and suggesting solutions that may allow them to stay well and continue contributing at work;
- Adopting psychologically safe approaches for settling disputes: Help to resolve workplace issues in a way that may be less confrontational or adversarial, especially for workers experiencing mental health issues;
- Addressing co-worker concerns: Work with the worker and employer to help ensure that co-worker concerns are addressed and working relationships are respectful;

- Supporting return to work: When a worker is returning to work after a mental health leave, it can be a critical time to support success. Proper planning can address potential issues including working relationships and performance, beginning while the worker is still off work;
- Ensuring confidentiality: Respect the worker's wishes about which information is kept private and what could be shared to help support a functioning workplace;
- Clarifying options: Help workers understand the options available to them in the accommodation process;
- Advocating and supporting: Help ensure that accommodation plans are focused on worker success in all situations, including when mental health needs to be taken into account;
- Supporting individual needs: Learn what will support the worker's safe and successful work accommodation and help ensure that the accommodation process respects the collective agreement;
- Following up: Periodically check in with the worker and employer to help ensure that the accommodation is working and make suggestions if adjustments are needed.

(Workplace Strategies for Mental Health, 2016)

The National Standard of Canada for Psychological Health and Safety in the Workplace and its accompanying tools introduced the first comprehensive guide in this area to the world. Canada's provinces are also now recognizing the importance of workplace psychological health and safety through their policies and laws.

References and Further Reading

Annex of National Standard of Canada on Psychological Health and Safety in the Workplace. (2013). *Sample audit tool.* Available at https://wsmh-cms.medir esource.com/wsmh/assets/nu49392rk7k8c48o. Accessed September 24, 2021.

Canada Life. (n.d.).Workplace strategies for mental health: Don't let chronic stress take its toll. Available at www.workplacestrategiesformentalhealth.com. Accessed September 24, 2021.

Canadian Centre for Occupational Health and Safety. (2021). OSH fact sheets: Mental health – psychosocial risk factors in the workplace. Available at www.ccohs.ca//oshanswers/psychosocial/mentalhealth_risk.html. Accessed September 19, 2021.

Collins, J. (2014). *Assembling the pieces: An implementation guide to the National Standard for Psychological Health and Safety in the Workplace.* CSA Group. Available at www.csagroup.org/store-resources/documents/codes-and-standards/SPE-Z1003-Guidebook.pdf. Accessed October 21, 2021.

CSA Group. (2013). CAN/CSA-Z1003-13/BNQ 9700-803/2013, Psychological health and safety in the workplace: Prevention, promotion, and guidance to staged implementation. Available at www.csagroup.org/store-resources/documents/codes-and-standards/2421865.pdf. Accessed September 24, 2021.

CSA Group. (2013). *Sample audit tool.* Available at https://wsmh-cms.mediresou rce.com/wsmh/assets/nu49392rk7k8c48o. Accessed September 24, 2021.

Great West Life. (n.d.). *Workplace strategies for mental health assessments: Sample audit tool.* Available at www.workplacestrategiesformentalhealth.com/resour ces/atw-assessments. Accessed July 29, 2021.

Guarding Minds@Work. (n.d.). Website. Available at www.guardingmindsatw ork.ca. Accessed September 24, 2021.

Ipsos Reid. (2017). Workplaces that are implementing the National Standard of Canada for Psychological Health and Safety in the Workplace described by employees as psychologically safer environments. Available at www.ipsos.com/ en-ca/news-polls/workplaces-implementing-national-standard-canada-psycho logical-health-and-safety-workplace. Accessed July 29, 2021.

Mental Health Commission of Canada. (2013). *National Standard of Canada for Psychological Health and Safety in the Workplace.* Available at www.men talhealthcommission.ca/English/what-we-do/workplace/national-standard. Accessed September 24, 2021.

Mental Health Commission of Canada. (2014). *Making the case for investing in mental health in Canada.* Available at www.mentalhealthcommission.ca/wp-content/uploads/drupal/2016-06/Investing_in_Mental_Health_FINAL_Vers ion_ENG.pdf. Accessed November 20, 2021.

Mental Health Commission of Canada. (2017). *Case Study Research Project findings: Final report.* Available at www.mentalhealthcommission.ca/wp-cont ent/uploads/drupal/2017-03/case_study_research_project_findings_2017_eng. pdf. Accessed September 19, 2021.

Samra, J., Gilbert, M., Shain, M. & Bilsker, D. (2009–2020). Know the psy-chosocial factors. Guarding Minds@Work, Simon Fraser University. Available at www.guardingmindsatwork.ca/about/about-psychosocial-factors. Accessed July 29, 2021.

Workplace Strategies for Mental Health. (2016). Union support for accommo-dation. Available at www.workplacestrategiesformentalhealth.com/resources/union-support-for-accommodation. Accessed July 29, 2021.

Workplace Strategies for Mental Health. (n.d.). Union and management cooper-ation. Available at www.workplacestrategiesformentalhealth.com/resources/union-and-management-cooperation. Accessed November 9, 2021.

Chapter 12

Australia's Steps to Address Psychological Health and Safety at Work

Work-related Stress

It is estimated that workplace stress affects around 32 percent of all Australians. (People at Work tool, n.d.).

Poor psychological health and safety and work-related psychological injury are expensive:

- The cost of workers' compensation claims relating to mental health (primary psychological workers' compensation claims) has increased by 80 percent, rising an average of 22 percent each year since 2017. Further, 80 percent of Australian employees surveyed want their employers to take action to address mental health in the workplace (Allianz, 2020).
- Work-related mental health conditions (also known as psychological injuries) have become a major concern in Australian workplaces due to the negative impact on individual employees, and the costs associated with the long periods away from work that are typical of these claims.
- Annually, 7,200 Australians are compensated for work-related mental health conditions, equating to around 6 percent of workers' compensation claims.
- Approximately $543 million is paid in workers' compensation for work-related mental health conditions each year.

(Safe Work Australia, n.d.).

Workplace Health and Safety Laws and Steps to Address Psychological Health at Work

Australia's workplace health and safety laws treat psychological hazards and risks as equivalent to physical hazards and risks.

Australia's Work Health and Safety (WHS) Act, effective in most jurisdictions, defines health to mean both physical and psychological

DOI: 10.4324/9781003187349-14

health. Persons conducting a business or undertaking, known as PCBUs (meaning the employer), have a duty of care that includes managing work-related risks to the psychological health of workers, so far as is reasonably practicable.

Psychological hazards are anything that increases the risk of work-related stress, including:

- High or low job demands;
- Low job control;
- Poor support;
- Poor workplace relationships;
- Low role clarity;
- Poor change management;
- Low reward and recognition;
- Poor organizational justice;
- Poor environmental conditions;
- Remote or isolated work; and
- Violent or traumatic events.

Australia has recently taken noteworthy steps to address psychological health at work. On May 20, 2021, Australia's state, territory, and Commonwealth ministers responsible for work health and safety agreed to a series of substantive amendments to the model WHS laws, including express provisions dealing with psychological injuries. Although the law considers health to mean both physical and psychological health, psychological health and safety has not been expressly provided for; however, the regulations are set to change.

The Boland Report: Psychological Health Identified as Priority Issue

Steps being taken by Australia to address psychological health and safety are largely a result of the 2018 final report of the Review of the Model Work Health and Safety Laws (the Boland Report).

The Boland Report[1] reviewed health and safety laws and offered recommendations designed to enhance Australia's WHS Framework. It recommends putting psychological health into regulations as a matter of priority by amending the model WHS Regulations to deal with identifying the psychosocial risks associated with psychological injury and the appropriate control measures to manage those risks (Safe Work Australia, 2018, p. 34):

> Ideas for strengthening the focus on workers' psychological health included calls for the model WHS Act to highlight psychosocial

risks in a similar way to physical risks, for the legislation to refer-ence risks associated with the 'psychological working environment' or workplace culture and hazardous workplace behaviours (similar to hazardous plant and substances), and for proactive supportive mechanisms for improving psychological health to be incorporated into the WHS laws.

(Safe Work Australia, 2018, pp. 31–32)

This inclusion of a psychological hazard regulation in the Model Work and Health Safety Act would require employers to treat hazards to mental health, such as stress, occupational violence, bullying, and sexual harassment, in the same way as physical hazards in the workplace by identifying specific risks and addressing them:

Recommendation 2: Make regulations dealing with psychological health. Amend the model WHS Regulations to deal with how to identify the psychosocial risks associated with psychological injury and the appropriate control measures to manage those risks.

(Safe Work Australia, 2018, pp. 8, 35)

The report found that employers are uncertain about the best way to address psychological health in the workplace:

Many stakeholders pointed to a lack of clarity about how to manage the risks to psychological health and identified this as problematic in light of rising rates of psychological injuries. Some criticised the absence of specific references to psychological health within the gen-eral duties, while others were wary of creating a separation between psychological and physical health.

(Safe Work Australia, 2018, pp. 31–32)

Submissions identified that many employers also find managing the risks to psychological health difficult:

Most feel that they lack the requisite expertise and are wary of inter-vening in case they do further harm. While the importance of workers' psychological health was unquestioned, some employer representatives queried the extent to which PCBUs should have responsibility for their workers' overall psychological wellbeing. While many submissions equated psychological harm with bullying and harassment, some emphasised the need to think more broadly about protecting workers' psychological health. There were differing views about the extent to which psychosocial risks could be "designed out" of the workplace.

(Safe Work Australia, 2018, p. 32)

Safe Work Australia: National Guidance on Work-related Psychological Health and Safety

Safe Work Australia, an Australian government statutory agency, published *Work-related Psychological Health and Safety: A Systematic approach to meeting your Duties—National Guidance Material* in June 2018, last updated January 2019.

The guidance provides a step-by-step process for managing psychological injury, by intervening early and taking preventative action to prevent workers becoming ill or sustaining a psychological injury. It sets forth a comprehensive listing of psychosocial hazards, stating that:

> Psychosocial hazards or factors are anything in the design or management of work that increases the risk of work-related stress. A stress response is the physical, mental and emotional reactions that occur when a worker perceives the demands of their work exceed their ability or resources to cope. Work-related stress if prolonged and/or severe can cause both psychological and physical injury.

Workers are likely to be exposed to a combination of psychosocial hazards; some may always be present, while others are present only occasionally.

Psychosocial Hazards and Factors

Common psychosocial hazards and factors include the following:

High Job Demands

This means sustained high physical, mental and/or emotional effort is required to do the job. Some examples are tasks or jobs that require:

- Long work hours;
- High workloads—too much to do, fast work pace or significant time pressure;
- Long periods of vigilance looking for infrequent events (such as air traffic controllers, long-distance drivers, security monitoring);
- Emotional effort in responding to distressing situations or distressed or aggressive clients (such as paramedics dealing with difficult patients);
- Exposure to traumatic events or work-related violence (such as emergency workers);
- Shiftwork leading to higher risk of fatigue;

- Frequently working in unpleasant or hazardous conditions (such as extreme temperatures or noise, around hazardous chemicals or dangerous equipment, or having to perform demanding work while wearing uncomfortable protective clothing or equipment).

Low Job Demands

This means sustained low levels of physical, mental, or emotional effort required to do the job, including tasks or jobs where there is:

- Too little to do;
- Highly repetitive or monotonous tasks (such as picking and packing products, monitoring production lines).

Low Job Control

This is where workers have little control over aspects of the work, including how or when a job is done; it applies to tasks or jobs where:

- Work is machine or computer paced;
- Work is tightly managed (as in scripted call centers);
- Workers have little say in the way they do their work, when they can take breaks, or when they can change tasks;
- Workers are not involved in decisions that affect them or their clients;
- Workers are unable to refuse to deal with aggressive clients (such as police officers).

Poor Support

This applies to tasks or jobs were workers have inadequate:

- Emotional support from supervisors and co-workers;
- Information or training to support their work performance; or
- Tools, equipment, and/or resources to do the job.

Poor Workplace Relationships

These can occur in jobs where there is:

- Workplace bullying, aggression, and harassment—including sexual harassment;
- Discrimination, or other unreasonable behaviors by co-workers, supervisors, or clients;

- Poor relationships between workers and their managers, supervisors, co-workers, and clients, or others with whom the worker is required to interact;
- Conflict between workers and their managers, supervisors or co-workers—this is made worse if managers are reluctant to deal with inappropriate behaviors;
- Lack of fairness and equity in dealing with organizational issues or where performance issues are poorly managed.

Low Role Clarity

This occurs in jobs where there is:

- Uncertainty about or frequent changes to tasks and work standards;
- Important task information that is not available to the worker;
- Conflicting job roles, responsibilities, or expectations (such as a worker being told one job is a priority, but another manager disagreeing).

Poor Organizational Change Management

This can happen in workplaces where there is:

- Insufficient consideration of the potential WHS and performance impacts during downsizing or relocations or associated with the introduction of new technology and production processes;
- Inadequate consultation and communication with key stakeholders and workers about major changes;
- Not enough practical support for workers during transitions times.

Low Recognition and Reward

This can be the case in jobs where:

- There is a lack of positive feedback;
- There is an imbalance between workers' efforts and formal and informal recognition and rewards;
- There is a lack of opportunity for skills development;
- Skills and experience are under-used.

Poor Organizational Justice

This can occur in workplaces where there is:

- Inconsistent application of policies and procedures;
- Unfairness or bias in decisions about allocation of resources and work;
- Poor management of under-performance.

Poor Environmental Conditions

This can involve exposure to poor-quality or hazardous working environments. Examples include:

- Hazardous manual tasks;
- Poor air quality;
- High noise levels;
- Extreme temperatures;
- Working near unsafe machinery.

Remote Work

Work at locations where access to resources and communications is difficult and travel times may be lengthy. Examples include farmers, real estate agents, a community nurse conducting visits at night, night shift operators in petrol stations or convenience stores, offshore mining, and fly-in, fly-out (FIFO) workers.

Isolated Work

This is work where there are no or few other people around, and where access to help from others—especially in an emergency—may be difficult.

Violent or Traumatic Events

A workplace incident may involve exposure to abuse, or the threat of or actual harm that causes fear and distress and can lead to stress and/or a physical injury. This is common among groups such as first responders, disaster and emergency services, and defense personnel. Examples include robbery, assault, being bitten, spat at, scratched or kicked, or being threatened with a weapon (Safe Work Australia, 2019, pp. 9–12).

Managing Work-related Psychological Health and Safety

The Guide provides a systematic and practical approach to managing work-related psychological health and safety, employing the phases of "preventing harm," "intervening early," and "supporting recovery" as follows:

Prevent harming

- Identify work-related hazards and risks;
- Assess risks (where the degree of risk and suitable controls are not already known);
- Implement effective control measures to eliminate hazards or minimise risks. The main focus on the good design and effective management of work, creating safe systems of work and ensuring appropriate communication and behaviour; and
- Consult effectively with your workers, their representatives and others where required.

Intervening early—Early identification and management of any risks can help minimise the potential severity of injuries and time lost from work.

- Review control measures and, where they are not effective, take action. The review might be prompted by routine monitoring or by your workers raising concerns about their psychological health and safety;
- Support workers showing early signs of work-related stress and modify their work duties to suit their circumstances; and
- Provide early assistance for individuals who have an increased risk of injury such as facilitating access to appropriate mental health services.

Supporting recovery—provide early assistance and support to access treatment and rehabilitation services, generally from the time a claim is lodged.

- Support timely and sustainable recovery at work (RAW) or return to work (RTW) through effective consultation, addressing any remaining work-related psychosocial hazards and risks that may exacerbate the existing work-related psychological injury or cause a new injury; and
- Review the effectiveness of the control measures to ensure further harm or new injury does not occur.

A fourth piece, called Inner Circle, is described by the guide as including important actions that should be occurring throughout the three stages and on an ongoing basis:

- Ensuring there is good work design and safe systems of work;
- Ensuring you are effectively controlling hazards and risks and monitoring and reviewing controls;
- Ensuring your workers have the training, information and supervision to do their job safely and well;
- Consulting with your workers and their health and safety representatives and consulting, co-operating and co-ordinating on any health and safety risks with all relevant people;
- Ensuring you, your leaders and management commit to WHS, including things required under WHS law and demonstrating due diligence.

(Safe Work Australia, 2019, pp. 5–6)

Identification

The Guide states that the first step in the risk management process is to identify all work-related psychosocial hazards. Psychosocial hazards may be identified by:

- Having conversations with workers, supervisors and health and safety specialists;
- Inspecting the workplace to see how work is carried out, noting any rushing, delays or work backlogs;
- Noticing how people interact with each other during work activities;
- Reviewing relevant information and records such as reporting systems including incident reports, workers' compensation claims, staff surveys, and absenteeism and staff turnover data;
- Using surveys to gather information from workers, supervisors and managers.

In complex situations, advice should be sought on specific risk identification and assessment techniques and seek the help of specialists.

Individual Workers

People respond to hazards in different ways. Individual differences that may make some workers more susceptible to harm from exposure to a hazard include:

- Being a new or young worker;
- Having an existing disability, injury, or illness;
- Having previously been exposed to a traumatic event; or
- Being a worker currently experiencing difficult personal circumstances.

By talking to these workers and learning how they are coping, it can be determined whether some additional support or adjustment may be necessary for them to perform their work safely.

Australia also discusses the duty that employers have to exercise due diligence to ensure they meet their WHS obligations:

Due diligence includes taking reasonable steps to do the following:

- Acquire and update knowledge of work-related psychological health and safety matters;
- Understand the organisation's operations, including any risks to work-related psychological health and safety;
- Ensure there are appropriate resources and processes to eliminate or manage risks, and these are used to effectively manage risks to psychological health;
- Ensure there are appropriate processes for receiving, monitoring and reviewing information on incidents, hazards and risks, and they are responded to in a timely way;
- Ensure the PCBU has processes for complying with any duties or obligations under WHS laws; and
- Verify resources and processes are provided and used to manage risk.

(Safe Work Australia, 2019, pp. 9–15)

Consulting Workers

Consultation is a key element of providing a psychologically healthy and safe work environment. The employer has a duty to consult with affected workers; if there is a health and safety representatives (HSR), the HSR must be included in the consultation.

Consultation on psychological health and safety matters involves:

- Sharing information on hazards and risks;
- Giving workers a reasonable opportunity to express their views, raise issues, and contribute to the decision-making process;
- Taking those views into account. It is important to respect their privacy and keep information confidential where this is necessary;
- Advising workers of the outcomes.

Consultation with workers and their HSRs is legally required, so far as reasonably practicable, at each step of the risk-management process. If workers are represented by unions, it is advisable to seek their input during the consultation process.

New South Wales Code of Practice on Managing Risks to Psychological Health

The New South Wales Government's Code of Practice on Managing Psychosocial Hazards at Work is *Australia's First Approved Code of Practice for Managing Psychosocial Hazards.*[2] It was developed by SafeWork NSW and issued in May 2021. The Code is intended to provide clear and practical guidance to organizations on how to identify and deal with psychological hazards such as role overload, role conflict, low job control, bullying, harassment, poor supervisor support, and isolated work. It was issued in response to concerning statistics demonstrating companies' difficulty in managing psychosocial issues and provides guidance on how to comply with the WHS duty to manage workplace risks that may contribute to psychological injuries or mental disorders.

Although non-mandatory, it is comprehensive and instructive, identifying common workplace psychosocial hazards and practical steps for addressing these hazards. It offers detailed information and practical measures on who has duties and what is involved in managing psychosocial hazards at work, responding to a report of psychosocial risk or incident, and supporting a safe return to work after a work-related harm, as well as example scenarios for managing psychosocial hazards and risks at work.

The Code is designed to supplement the WHS Act protections and does not increase the existing duties under work health and safety (WHS) laws, but rather aims to clarify an organization's responsibilities and obligations with regard to addressing workplace psychosocial hazards that may potentially cause psychological or physical harm. The Code is applicable to all NSW workplaces and industries.

The Code notes that a common failure in the existing psychological risk-management process is to focus on poor behavior between individuals, rather than implementing controls that target the source of the stressor(s):

> Psychosocial hazards at work are aspects of work and situations that may cause a stress response which in turn can lead to psychological or physical harm. These stem from:
>
> - The way the tasks or job are designed, organised, managed and supervised,
> - Tasks or jobs where there are inherent psychosocial hazards and risks,
> - The equipment, working environment or requirements to undertake duties in physically hazardous environments, and
> - Social factors at work, workplace relationships and social interactions.

Psychosocial hazards and the appropriate controls will vary for every workplace and sometimes between groups of workers.

(NSW Government, 2021)

A four-step process is outlined to manage psychosocial hazards:

- Step 1: Identify the psychosocial hazards;
- Step 2: Assess and prioritize the psychosocial hazards and risks;
- Step 3: Control psychosocial hazards and risks;
- Step 4: Proactively implement, maintain, monitor, and review the effectiveness of controls.

Also observe and talk to workers about work activities.

If conducting a workplace survey, provide workers the option to respond anonymously.

Supporting a Safe Return to Work After a Work-related Harm

The Code states that:

When someone is returning to work, they may also be exposed to new and or different psychosocial or physical hazards (because they are doing different duties or working in a new worksite). The PCBU must proactively manage any new WHS risks which arise for the injured worker and the work group arising from the return-to-work process and the changed duties or work locations.

(NSW Government, 2021, p. 26)

It is also important to be aware that an employee may be returning to the same stressful circumstances. Appendix A Example Scenarios for Managing Psychosocial Hazards and Risks at Work, states:

The control measures you choose must suit the organisational and worker needs and effectively control the risks to the highest level that is reasonably practicable. The tables below outline ten scenarios with common psychosocial hazards and risks, example controls and approaches to maintain, monitor, review and achieve continual improvement of the risk management approach.

(NSW Government, 2021)

WorkSafe Victoria Preventing and Managing Work-related Stress: A Guide for Employers

Victoria's *WorkSafe Victoria: Preventing and Managing Work-related Stress: A Guide for Employers*, published in February 2021, provides guidance to employers to help them identify, eliminate, or reduce and manage the risk of work-related stress.

Practical steps are set out in the guide for employers to consider when managing PSHs contributing to work-related stress, as well as for a risk-management approach to work-related stress, implementation of a work-related stress management process, and early intervention for work-related stress.

The guide recommends that employers should lead by example and develop a culture of safety that is consistent with employers' obligations under workplace health and safety laws. The guide also addresses working from home.

This guide also offers comprehensive definitions, examples, and measures with regard to work-related stress and PSHs (WorkSafe Victoria, 2021).

SafeWork SA's People at Work Tool: Validated Psychosocial Risk Assessment Tool

SafeWork SA monitors work health and safety systems in relation to psychosocial risks in the workplace.

Inspectors visit workplaces to ensure that businesses are managing the risks associated with psychological safety in the workplace and have safe systems in place. SafeWork SA's primarily focus is on assisting and guiding businesses in understanding their obligations and ensuring that risks to workers' psychological health arising from inappropriate workplace behaviors are being managed appropriately.

SafeWork SA's Executive Director, Martyn Campbell, states that planned audits are a reminder for businesses to take psychological safety as seriously as workers physical safety:

> Employers have a responsibility to provide a safe and healthy workplace and this extends to psychological safety, not only physical safety ... Like all work health and safety hazards, these risks need to be managed in accordance with WHS legislative requirements.
>
> (SafeWork SA, 2021)

People at Work, Australia's only validated psychosocial risk assessment survey and tool, was launched by Campbell in February 2021. It helps organizations to identify, assess, and control risks to psychological health and safety. Campbell states that it does not need an expert to interpret the psychosocial risk assessment results. It is available free of charge.

A survey is conducted using the following questions:

- Core modules:
  - Your job and workplace (e.g., job demands – workplace factors that can cause stress; and job resources – workplace factors that can protect you from stress);
  - Workplace bullying;
  - Psychological health (e.g., psychological distress and burnout).
- Elective modules:
  - Work-related violence and aggression;
  - Sprain and strain;
  - Worker intentions (e.g., turnover and sick leave intentions).

Survey results are generated via a People at Work account, and an action plan is implemented accordingly. It is recommended that workplaces repeat the People at Work process on a regular basis, such as every 12 to 18 months.

The psychosocial hazards and factors in the People at Work survey include emotional demands, role ambiguity, role conflict, role overload, group relationship conflict, group task conflict, job control, supervisor support, co-worker support, praise and recognition, procedural justice, change consultation, workplace bullying, and work-related violence and aggression (People at Work, n.d.).

Other Relevant Developments

SafeWork NSW's Mentally Healthy Workplaces Strategy

This strategy, updated and relaunched in May 2021, aims to improve workplace mental health in response to significant shifts in ways of working due to COVID-19. During the pandemic, SafeWork NSW received more than 5,000 calls for assistance and information in relation to bullying and other psychosocial risks as well as how to get started in creating a mentally healthy workplace. The NSW Mentally Healthy Workplaces Strategy is the government's plan to support NSW employers, leaders and workers to take effective action to create mentally healthy workplaces. (NSW Government, 2020)

Psychosocial Health and Safety and Bullying in Australian Workplaces (6th Edition)

This sixth annual national statement was issued by Safe Work Australia in June 2021 to identify trends in psychosocial health and safety, and bullying in Australian workplaces. Results are based on workers' compensation claims due to mental stress in Australian workplaces, which offer a source of information about the psychosocial health and safety status of Australian workplaces (Safe Work Australia, 2021).

The Respect@Work report

In April 2021, the Australian Commonwealth Government released *A Roadmap for Respect: Preventing and Addressing Sexual Harassment in Australian Workplaces (Government Response)* in response to the Safety@Work report. The government agreed with recommendation 35 of the Safety@Work report that the Model WHS Regulation should be amended to deal with psychological health and that guidelines should be drafted with a view to creating a Code of Practice dealing with sexual harassment.

The foreword states:

> Our response to the Respect@Work Inquiry is about creating a new culture of respectful behaviour in Australian workplaces. A respectful culture should be commonplace. It should be business as usual. But the findings of the Sex Discrimination Commissioner's Respect@ Work Inquiry demonstrate that too many workplace cultures fall short.
>
> (Australian Government, 2021, p. 1)

Notably, the Respect@Work report states that, "There is an urgent need to raise awareness that sexual harassment is a work health and safety issue" (Australian Human Rights Commission, 2020).

The Fair Work Amendment (Respect at Work) Regulations 2021

These Regulations, effective on July 10, 2021, support amendments that would be made by the Sex Discrimination and Fair Work (Respect at Work) Amendment Bill 2021 to include sexual harassment in the existing anti-bullying jurisdiction by allowing an employee who has been sexually harassed at work to apply to the Fair Work Commission for an order to stop the sexual harassment (Australian Government, 2022).

Victoria's Proposed Occupational Health and Safety Amendment (Psychological Health) Regulations

Victoria opened a public consultation in February 2022 on proposed OHS regulations to provide clearer guidance to employers on their obligations to safeguard workers from mental injury.

WorkSafe Executive Director of Health and Safety Narelle Beer stated:

> These proposed regulations will put psychosocial hazards on equal footing with physical hazards and recognise that they can be just as harmful to employees' safety and wellbeing.
>
> (WorkSafe Victoria, 2022)

Comments were due by March 31, 2022. The proposed OHS Amendment (Psychological Health) Regulations are available at https://engage.vic.gov.au/proposed-psychological-health-regulations.

Notes

1 The Boland report was the first national review of the Model Work Health and Safety (WHS) Laws and was undertaken at the request of ministers with responsibility for WHS matters, who agreed that the content and operation of the Model WHS Laws would be reviewed every five years.
2 A Code of Practice provides detailed information on achieving the standards required under the work health and safety (WHS) laws. A code of practice is not mandatory, and duty holders may follow other approaches if they can demonstrate that, by following these, they can meet or exceed the minimum safety standards. Codes of practice are admissible in court proceedings.

References and Further Reading

Allianz. (2020). *Future thriving workplaces report: The rising cost of workplace mental health injuries.* Available at www.allianz.com.au/images/internet/allianz-au/ContentImages/Allianz_Future%20Thriving%20Workplaces%20report.pdf. Accessed November 17, 2021.

Australian Government, Federal Register of Legislation. (2022). *Fair Work Amendment (Respect at Work) Regulations.* Available at www.legislation.gov.au/Details/F2021L00972. Accessed July 17, 2021.

Australian Government. (2021). *A roadmap for respect: Preventing and addressing sexual harassment in Australian workplaces.* Available at www.ag.gov.au/sites/default/files/2021-04/roadmap-respect-preventing-addressing-sexual-harassment-australian-workplaces.pdf. Accessed November 9, 2021.

Australian Human Rights Commission. (2020). *Respect@Work: Sexual Harassment National Inquiry report.* Available at https://humanrights.gov.au/our-work/sex-discrimination/publications/respectwork-sexual-harassment-national-inquiry-report-2020#PHGSk. Accessed May 13, 2021.

Communique. (2021, May 20). Meeting of Work Health and Safety Ministers. Available at www.ag.gov.au/sites/default/files/2021-05/communique-meeting-WHS-ministers-20-may-2021.pdf. Accessed November 9, 2021.

Flourish Dx. (2021). *Psych Health and Safety Podcast*, episodes 1–95.

Hospital and Healthcare. (2020). The rising cost of workplace mental health injuries. Available at www.hospitalhealth.com.au/content/aged-allied-health/article/the-rising-cost-of-workplace-mental-health-injuries-796345406#axzz6jNosLFc8. Accessed October 31, 2021.

NSW Government. (2021). *Code of Practice: Managing Psychosocial Hazards at Work*. Sydney: Safework NSW. Available at www.safework.nsw.gov.au/__data/assets/pdf_file/0004/983353/Code-of-Practice_Managing-psychosocial-hazards.pdf. Accessed November 10, 2021.

NSW Government. (2020). *Mentally Healthy Workplaces Strategy*. Available at www.mentalhealthatwork.nsw.gov.au/committing-to-leading-change/the-strategy. Accessed November 2, 2021.

People at Work. (2021). Psychosocial hazards and factors. Available at www.peopleatwork.gov.au. Accessed October 31, 2021.

People at Work. (n.d.). *People at Work Tool*. Available at www.peopleatwork.gov.au/webcopy/businesscase. Accessed November 9, 2021.

Safe Work Australia. (2018). *Review of the Model Work Health and Safety laws: Final report [Boland Report]*. Available at www.safeworkaustralia.gov.au/system/files/documents/1902/review_of_the_model_whs_laws_final_report_0.pdf. Accessed September 21, 2021.

Safe Work Australia. (2021) Infographic: Four steps to preventing psychological injury at work. Available at www.safeworkaustralia.gov.au/doc/infographic-four-steps-preventing-psychological-injury-work. Accessed November 16, 2021.

Safe Work Australia. (2021). *Psychosocial health and safety and bullying in Australian workplaces* (6th edn). Available at www.safeworkaustralia.gov.au/doc/psychosocial-health-and-safety-and-bullying-australian-workplaces-6th-edition?utm_source=miragenews&utm_medium=miragenews&utm_campaign=news. Accessed June 11, 2021.

Safe Work Australia. (2019). *Work-related psychological health and safety: A systematic approach to meeting your duties—national guidance material*. Available at www.safeworkaustralia.gov.au/system/files/documents/1911/work-related_psychological_health_and_safety_a_systematic_approach_to_meeting_your_duties.pdf. Accessed September 15, 2021.

Safe Work Australia. (2021). *Preventing workplace sexual harassment—national guidance material*. Available at www.safeworkaustralia.gov.au/sites/default/files/2021-01/Guide%20for%20preventing%20workplace%20sexual%20harassment%20-%20for%20publishing.pdf. Accessed July 21, 2021.

Safe Work Australia. (n.d.). Mental health. Available at www.safeworkaustralia.gov.au/topic/mental-health#:~:text=7%2C200%20Australians%20are%20compensated%20for Accessed November 2, 2021.

SafeWork SA. (2021). Keeping workplaces psychologically healthy. Available at www.safework.sa.gov.au/news-and-alerts/news/news/2021/keeping-workplaces-psychologically-healthy. Accessed October 31, 2021.

WorkSafe Victoria. (2021). *Preventing and managing work-related stress: A guide for employers*. Available at www.worksafe.vic.gov.au/preventing-and-managing-work-related-stress-guide-employers. Accessed October 25, 2021.

WorkSafe Victoria. (2022). Psychological health regulations open for comment. Available at www.worksafe.vic.gov.au/news/2022-02/psychological-health-regulations-open-comment. Accessed May 6, 2022.

Chapter 13

Japan
Long Working Hours and Psychosocial Stress Check Screening

Work stress is a growing issue in the Asia Pacific, a region combining some of the richest countries as well as some of the poorest, and containing both advanced industrialized countries and developing economies. Long working hours are a significant issue in Japan, Korea, Taiwan, and China, resulting in occupational diseases and occasionally, sudden death.

The Danger of Long Working Hours

Long working hours are a psychosocial hazard. On May 17, 2021, the World Health Organization (WHO) and International Labour Organization (ILO) issued the first global analysis of the loss of life and health associated with working long hours. It found that working 55 hours or more per week is a serious health hazard; specifically, long working hours led to 745,000 deaths from stroke and ischemic heart disease in 2016, a 29 percent increase since 2000.

The WHO and ILO estimate that, in 2016, 398 000 people died from stroke and 347,000 from heart disease as a result of having worked at least 55 hours a week. Between 2000 and 2016, the number of deaths from heart disease due to working long hours increased by 42 percent, and from stroke by 19 percent".

> [The] work-related disease burden is particularly significant in men (72% of deaths occurred among males), people living in the Western Pacific and South-East Asia regions, and middle-aged or older workers. Most of the deaths recorded were among people dying aged 60–79 years, who had worked for 55 hours or more per week between the ages of 45 and 74 years. With working long hours now known to be responsible for about one-third of the total estimated work-related burden of disease, it is established as the risk factor with the largest occupational disease burden. This shifts thinking

DOI: 10.4324/9781003187349-15

towards a relatively new and more psychosocial occupational risk factor to human health.

(WHO & ILO, 2021)

The World Health Organization states that the following actions to protect workers' health can be taken:

- Governments can introduce, implement and enforce laws and policies that ban mandatory overtime and ensure maximum limits on working time;
- Collective bargaining agreements between employers and workers' associations can arrange for more flexible working time as well as agreeing on a maximum number of working hours;
- Employees might share working hours to ensure that the number of hours worked do not rise to 55 or more per week.

(WHO & ILO, 2021)

Japan and Long Work Hours

In Japan, *karōshi* means death from overwork or work-related stress, and it is a growing problem. Leading causes of *karōshi* include strokes, heart disease, severe cases of asthma, and suicide, or death by overwork. This term dates to the late 1970s, when Japanese doctors began using it to describe sudden mortality due to the stress of excessive work. In December 2016, in response to the highly publicized suicide of a young employee at advertising giant Dentsu, Japan's Ministry of Health, Labor, and Welfare released emergency guidelines aimed at preventing *karōshi*.

Karoshi *Hotline and Work Style Reform*

The Japan Times reported that a legal aid group received 206 consultation calls in one day about suicide and death from overwork after launching a hotline in June 2020 to deal with the problem. In 81 cases, callers expressed fears that they could be forced to work until death.

Japan has introduced an Act on the Arrangement of Related Acts to Promote Work Style Reform in 2018. This law requires employers to develop an environment that allows employees to work according to their willingness and capabilities with an awareness of work–life balance. Measures to take include putting in place a maximum limit on overtime, shortening the prescribed working hours, and improving other working conditions (METI, 2018).

Japan's National Policy for Psychosocial Stress Screening

Japan's Stress Check Program, a national policy for monitoring and screening psychosocial stress in the workplace, is designed to help prevent stress in response to an epidemic of stress-related death and disease. Launched by the Japanese government in December 2015, the program is a national occupational health policy to screen employees for high psychosocial stress in the workplace. The program mandates that all workplaces with 50 or more employees conduct a Stress Check for workers at least once a year.

The Stress Check Program is unique compared with the global trend for psychosocial risk management because it focuses on the assessment of stress in individual workers.

The Stress Check Program includes two main components for the primary prevention of mental health problems among workers:

- An annual stress survey, which aims to decrease the risk of mental health problems in workers by increasing their awareness of their own stress through periodic surveys and feedback;
- An analysis of group stress survey results to identify work-related stressors, followed by active efforts to improve the psychosocial work environment in order to improve the psychosocial work environment based on group analysis of data collected by the stress surveys.

Employers are required to offer the Stress Check, but workers are not required to participate. Employers can use alternative questionnaires but are required to include the same domains of workplace stressors, symptoms, and support.

The 57-question assessment tool addresses topics including workload, amount of control over job and workload management, personal physical and mental health, and satisfaction with job and family life.

The Brief Job Stress Questionnaire—English Version

Answer the questions concerning the job by circling the number that best fitting the situation: 1) Very much so; 2) Moderately so; 3) Somewhat; 4) Not at all.

1. I have an extremely large amount of work to do.
2. I can't complete work in the required time.
3. I have to work as hard as I can.
4. I have to pay very careful attention.

5. My job is difficult in that it requires a high level of knowledge and technical skill.
6. I need to be constantly thinking about work throughout the working day.
7. My job requires a lot of physical work.
8. I can work at my own pace.
9. I can choose how and in what order to do my work.
10. I can reflect my opinions on workplace policy.
11. My knowledge and skills are rarely used at work.
12. There are differences of opinion within my department.
13. My department does not get along well with other departments.
14. The atmosphere in my workplace is friendly.
15. My working environment is poor (e.g., noise, lighting, temperature, ventilation).
16. This job suits me well.
17. My job is worth doing.
18. I have been very active.
19. I have been full of energy.
20. I have been lively.
21. I have felt angry.
22. I have been inwardly annoyed or aggravated.
23. I have felt irritable.
24. I have felt extremely tired.
25. I have felt exhausted.
26. I have felt weary or listless.
27. I have felt tense.
28. I have felt worried or insecure.
29. I have felt restless.
30. I have been depressed.
31. I have thought that doing anything was a hassle.
32. I have been unable to concentrate.
33. I have felt gloomy.
34. I have been unable to handle work.
35. I have felt sad.
36. I have felt dizzy.
37. I have experienced joint pains.
38. I have experienced headaches.
39. I have had a stiff neck and/or shoulders.
40. I have had lower back pain.
41. I have had eyestrain.
42. I have experienced heart palpitations or shortness of breath.
43. I have experienced stomach and / or intestine problems.
44. I have lost my appetite.

45. I have experienced diarrhea and/or constipation.
46. I haven't been able to sleep well.

(Ministry of Health, Labour and Welfare, n.d.)

The law mandates that employees be given the results of their Stress Check. Those found to be at high risk for potentially harmful stress are referred to a physician.

Employers are required to modify stressful work conditions, such as schedules, work location, or responsibilities, in collaboration with high-risk employees' physicians.

While not mandated, employers are also encouraged to analyze the data from the stress survey on a team basis and improve the psycho-social work environment based on the analysis. Measures that might be implemented include reducing work hours, improving ways to work, and improving communication in the workplace. Specific interventions are not prescribed, but models and case studies are available.

The release of employees' data to employers without the employees' permission is prohibited, as is discrimination based on Stress Check participation or results.

Evidence indicates that the Stress Check questionnaire does identify people who are at high risk of mental health-related disability and supports organizational change more than personal interventions to prevent worker stress. It is thought that combining the annual stress survey with improvements in the psychosocial work environment may effectively reduce psychological distress.

References and Further Reading

Dollard, M. F., Shimazu, A., Nordin, R. B., Brough, P. & Tuckey, M. R. (2014). *Psychosocial factors at work in the Asia Pacific*. New York: Springer.

Hiroshi, K. (2017, June 2). Confronting *karōshi*: Actions to prevent death from overwork. Nippon.com. Available at www.nippon.com/en/currents/d00310/#. Accessed September 24, 2021.

Japan Times. (2000, June 18,). *Karoshi* hotline flooded on first day. Available at www.japantimes.co.jp/news/2000/06/18/national/karoshi-hotline-flooded-on-first-day. Accessed September 24, 2021.

Jozito. (n.d.) Japan gets real about workplace stress. Available at www.jozito.com/japan-gets-real-about-workplace-stress. Accessed September 24, 2021.

METI. (2018). *Act on the Arrangement of Related Acts to Promote Work Style Reform*. Available at www.mhlw.go.jp/english/policy/employ-labour/labour-standards/dl/201904kizyun.pdf. Accessed November 4, 2021.

Ministry of Health, Labour and Welfare. (n.d.). *The Brief Job Stress Questionnaire (BJSQ), English version*. Available at www.mhlw.go.jp/bunya/roudoukijun/anzeneisei12/dl/160621-1.pdf. Accessed September 22, 2021.

National Defense Counsel for Victims of *Karoshi*. (n.d.). No more *karoshi*. Available at https://karoshi.jp/english. Accessed November 12, 2021.

Tsutsumi, A., Shimazu, A., Eguchi, H., Inoue, A. & Kawakami, N. (2018). A Japanese Stress Check Program screening tool predicts employee long-term sickness absence: a prospective study. *Journal of Occupational Health* 60(1), 55–63.

WHO & ILO. (2021). Long working hours increasing deaths from heart disease and stroke: WHO, ILO. Available at www.who.int/news/item/17-05-2021-long-working-hours-increasing-deaths-from-heart-disease-and-stroke-who-ilo. Accessed September 22, 2021.

Chapter 14

Global Standard on Psychological Health and Safety at Work

ISO 45003: First Global Standard on Psychological Health and Safety at Work

Global Standard ISO 45003 Psychological Health and Safety in the Workplace is the first global standard that helps organizations identify and control work-related hazards and manage psychosocial risks within an occupational health and safety management system.

ISO 45003 was published on June 9, 2021 by the International Organization for Standardization (ISO), a worldwide federation of national standards bodies. The Standard is the product of 74 countries coming together with the goal of making the workplace more psychologically safe and healthy.

It covers both physical health and safety and broader mental wellbeing, and ensures that progress is measurable. ISO 45003 is a voluntary standard.

ISO 45003 Highlights

Much of ISO 45003 sets out how psychosocial hazards (PSH) arise, addressing how the workplace is organized, the social factors at work, and the work environment itself. It offers practical guidance around the management of psychological health, including how to recognize hazards linked to working remotely.

Guidance is provided to organizations on how to:

- Identify the conditions, circumstances, and workplace demands that have the potential to impair the psychological health and wellbeing of employees;
- Identify primary risk factors and assess them to determine what changes are required to improve the working environment;

DOI: 10.4324/9781003187349-16

- Identify and control work-related hazards and manage psychosocial risk within an occupational health and safety (OH&S) management system.

ISO 450003 addresses areas that can impact a worker's psychological health, including ineffective communication, excessive pressure, poor leadership, and organizational culture. It focuses more on root causes of issues and organizational change than individual resilience or interventions. The standard provides examples of what can be done to eliminate or manage psychosocial risks. It is written in such a way to be accessible to everyone, including those without expertise.

ISO 450003 prioritizes people:

> [It] addresses the many areas that can impact a worker's psychological health, including ineffective communication, excessive pressure, poor leadership and organizational culture. The standard covers aspects such as how to identify the conditions, circumstances and workplace demands that have the potential to impair the psychological health and wellbeing of workers; how to identify primary risk factors and assess them to determine what changes are required to improve the working environment; and how to identify and control work-related hazards and manage psychosocial risk within an occupational health and safety management system.
>
> (Naden, 2021)

Specific information is included on:

- What psychosocial risks are—through guidance on how to identify the conditions, circumstances, and workplace demands that have the potential to harm the psychological health and safety of employees (see Chapter 2 for a comprehensive list and examples of psychosocial hazards drawn from ISO 45003);
- How to identify, assess, and manage them to improve the working environment;
- The impact of PSH on the organization and employee.

Top Management Commitment

ISO 45003 expressly calls for top management involvement, stating that successful management of psychosocial risk calls for a commitment throughout the organization.

ISO 45003 emphasizes the importance of leadership and commitment:

> The successful management of psychosocial risk calls for a commitment throughout the organization. Top management should

lead this, and managers and workers at all levels should assist in its implementation.

(ISO, 2021)

ISO 45003 also states that top management is responsible for the functioning of the occupational health and safety management system and should clarify roles, responsibilities and authorities for managing psychosocial risk in the workplace (ISO, 2021, 5.3)

ISO 45003 calls upon top management to take the following steps:

a) Demonstrate leadership and commitment to managing psycho-social risk and to promoting wellbeing at work;
b) Identify, monitor and be aware of its roles and responsibilities with respect to managing psychosocial risks;
c) Determine the resources needed and make them available in a timely and efficient manner;
d) Reinforce the sustainability of managing psychosocial risk by including it in strategic plans and existing systems, processes and reporting structures;
e) Protect workers from reprisals and/or threats of reprisals for reporting incidents, hazards, risks and opportunities;
f) Communicate how whistle-blowers, victims, witnesses and those who report or raise workplace psychosocial risk concerns will be protected;
g) Obtain and provide feedback to determine the effectiveness of managing and preventing psychosocial risk within the OH&S management system, both in implementation and operation;
h) Empower workers and ensure they are competent to fulfil their roles and responsibilities to identify and manage psycho-social risk;
i) Remove barriers that can limit worker participation, and aim to enhance participation;
j) Actively engage workers in a continual dialogue on the management of psychosocial risk;
k) Support and encourage workers to actively participate in the management of psychosocial risk in the workplace.

(ISO, 2021, 5.1)

Prioritizing People: Consideration of Worker Needs and Expectations

The Standard states that, in relation to managing psychosocial risk, the organization should understand and determine the needs and expectations of workers and other interested parties.

Workers and other interested parties have a range of needs and expectations that can be influenced by psychosocial risks at work. These needs and expectations can include:

- financial security;
- social interaction and support;
- inclusion, recognition, rew5ard and accomplishment;
- personal development and growth;
- equal opportunity and fair treatment at work.

(ISO, 2021, 4.2)

Participation and Consultation of Workers

ISO 45003 calls for engaging, empowering, and supporting workers in their roles and responsibilities in terms of managing PSH at work. The employer should determine the resources employees need and make them available in a timely and efficient manner. Employees should be protected from reprisal when reporting incidents, hazards, risks, and opportunities. The employer should also communicate how all those raising issues of psychosocial risks and concerns will be protected.

An employer's main obligations include the following:

- Establish and maintain to employees a psychosocial risk prevention policy;
- Identify psychosocial risk factors and evaluate the organizational environment (applicable to workplaces with more than 50 employees);
- Use questionnaires to identify psychosocial risk factors (applicable to workplaces with 16–50 employees);
- Distribute to employees the policy and measures adopted to reduce psychosocial risks;
- Identify the employees subject to psychosocial damages while working or derived from their work;
- Provide a registry where employees can learn about psychosocial risk factors and corrective actions taken;
- Maintain a confidential complaint system so the employees can inform the employer about psychosocial risk factors; and
- Take actions to prevent psychosocial risk factors and corrective measures if psychosocial damage occurs.

(ISO, 2021, 6.2)

International Standards: ISO 45001 and ISO 45003: Management of Psychosocial Risks at Work as Part of an Occupational Health and Safety Management(OHS) System

ISO 45003 places psychosocial risks within the OHS management system. ISO 45003 guidance follows the structure of ISO 45001, so the two standards can be used together.

ISO 45003 is intended to be used together with ISO 45001, an OHS management system with the intention of providing healthy and safe workplaces. It is written to be accessible to everyone, including those without expertise. ISO 45003 is applicable to organizations of all sizes and in all sectors for the development, implementation, maintenance, and continual improvement of safe and healthy workplaces.

OSH Management System 45001: 2018 Occupational Health and Safety Management Systems—Requirements with Guidance for Use (ISO 45001)[1]

ISO 45001 uses a business imperative for promoting and protecting the physical and psychological health and safety of workers. ISO 45001 certification helps the employer provide a framework for the health, safety, and wellbeing of employees.

ISO 45003 is a child standard of the ISO 45001 standard and elaborates on these elements referred to in ISO 45001 with regard to how to identify and control work-related hazards and manage psychosocial risks within an occupational health and safety management system.

Taken together, these Standards aim to prevent injury and ill-health to workers and to provide a safe and healthy workplace.

ISO45003 is intended to fit into an existing OHS system rather than to be a stand-alone OHS system to manage PSH, but it can also be used on its own.

Companies designing OHS management systems using ISO 45001 will not be required to design a new system for ISO 45003. While ISO 45003 is a stand-alone system, it can be incorporated into companies using ISO 45001.

The British Standards Institution (BSI, 2021) states that:

> ISO 45003 is written to help organizations using an occupational health and safety management system based on ISO 45001 Occupational Health and Safety. It will also be useful for organizations that haven't yet implemented an occupational health and safety management system.

BSI offers a one-minute YouTube video on the Standard, available at https://youtu.be/qK2QPCeXGiA.

The user of ISO 45003 does not have to be an expert or a psychologist, and may take the action of calling in outside resources or experts. The guidance provided on protecting psychological health by managing psychosocial risk within an OHS management system aims to help organizations manage this complex and important aspect of OHS and promote wellbeing at work. The standard can be used by human resources, line managers, and OHS.

ISO 450003 has the potential to change how organizations view psychological health and safety. The credibility of a global standard in the psychosocial health and safety management area will hopefully encourage organizations, in consultation with their leaders and employees, to address this increasingly important workplace issue. ISO 45003 helps signal that psychological health and safety is no longer just a human resources issue, but an OHS one as well.

Note

1   ISO 45001 builds on the success of earlier international standards in this area, such as OHSAS 18001, the International Labour Organization's ILO-OSH Guidelines, various national standards and the ILO's International Labour Standards and Conventions. ISO 45001:2018 was published on March 12, 2018, and OHSA's 18001 was withdrawn on March 12, 2021.

References and Further Reading

BSI. (2021). *ISO 45003 Psychological Health and Safety at Work*. Available at www.bsigroup.com/en-AU/iso-45003. Accessed 21 November 2021.

Foulis, M. (2021, July 19). New standard to raise the bar on psychological safety, by Maia Foulis. Canadian Occupational Safety. Available at www. thesafetymag.com/ca/topics/psychological-safety/new-standard-to-raise-the-bar-on-psychological-safety/276292?utm_source=GA&utm_medium=20210 719&utm_campaign=COSW-Newsletter-20210719&utm_content=A6EBC 887-D312-4906-A2F3-B036EDBEAAAA&tu=A6EBC887-D312-4906-A2F3-B036EDBEAAAA. Accessed July 20, 2021.

International Organization for Standardization (ISO). (2021). *ISO 45003: 2021 Occupational Health and Safety Management—Psychological Health and Safety at Work—Guidelines for Managing Psychosocial Risks*. Available at www.iso.org/obp/ui/#iso:std:iso:45003:ed-1:v1:en. Accessed October 28, 2021.

Naden, C. (2021). Mental health in the workplace. International Organization for Standardization (ISO). Available at www.iso.org/news/ref2677.html. Accessed June 29, 2021.

World Health Organization. (2007, July). *The Global Occupational Health Network special issue: Addressing psychosocial risks and work-related stress in countries in economic transition, in newly industrialized countries, and in developing countries.* Available at www.who.int/occupational_health/publicati ons/newsletter/gohnetspecial072007.pdf. Accessed November 10, 2021.

Chapter 15

Developing Countries and International Conventions

Work-related stress is an issue of growing concern in developing countries. Globalization and the changing nature of work are accompanied by significant work-related stress. However, in less developed countries there may be a lack of awareness of work-related stress and a shortage of resources to deal with it.

Cultural aspects also need to be considered when dealing with work-related stress in developing countries.

Developing Countries and Stress

In developing countries, large organizations may look to international standards and conventions such as ISO 45003, discussed earlier, or Convention 190, discussed below, to build codes of conduct, policies, and employee handbooks.

ILO Convention 190: First International Legal Standard Addressing Workplace Harassment and Violence

The ILO adopted Convention 190, Eliminating Violence and Harassment in the World of Work, referred to as the Violence and Harassment Convention, 2019, on June 21, 2019. This Convention is the first international treaty on violence and harassment in the world of work. It became effective in June 2021 and is an international legally binding instrument.

In adopting the Convention, the ILO acknowledged that violence and harassment in the world of work affect a person's psychological, physical, and sexual health, dignity, and family and social environment. It also recognizes the importance of a work culture based on mutual respect and dignity of the human being to prevent violence and harassment.

DOI: 10.4324/9781003187349-17

Broad Definition of Violence and Harassment

For the purpose of the Convention, violence and harassment in the world of work refer to a range of unacceptable behaviors and practices, or threats—whether a single occurrence or repeated—that aim at, result in, or are likely to result in physical, psychological, sexual, or economic harm. Gender-based violence and harassment are included in this definition.

Scope

This Convention protects workers and other persons in the world of work, including employees as defined by national law and practice, as well as workers regardless of their contractual status; those in training, such as interns and apprentices; workers whose employment has been terminated; volunteers, jobseekers, and job applicants; and individuals exercising the authority, duties, or responsibilities of an employer.

Application

The Convention applies to violence and harassment in the world of work occurring in the course of, linked with, or arising out of work:

- In the workplace, including public and private spaces where they are a place of work;
- In places where the worker is paid, takes a rest break or a meal, or uses sanitary, washing, and changing facilities;
- During work-related trips, travel, training, events, or social activities;
- Through work-related communications, including those enabled by information and communication technologies;
- In employer-provided accommodation;
- When commuting to and from work.

ILO Convention 190 and Psychosocial Hazards

Convention 190 calls upon each member state to adopt laws and regulations requiring employers to take appropriate steps to prevent violence and harassment in the world of work, including, so far as is reasonably practicable, taking into account violence and harassment and associated psychosocial risks in the management of occupational safety and health; and identifying hazards and assessing risks of violence and harassment, taking into account factors that increase the likelihood of violence and harassment, including psychosocial hazards and risks.

Particular attention should be paid to hazards and risks that arise from working conditions and arrangements, work organization and human resource management, as appropriate; involve third parties such as clients, customers, service providers, users, patients and members of the public; and arise from discrimination, abuse of power relations, and gender, cultural, and social norms that support violence and harassment.

Countries that have ratified Convention 190 include Argentina, Italy, Ecuador, South Africa, Namibia, Somalia, Uruguay, and the United Kingdom.

References and Further Reading

Houtman, I. & Jettinghoff, K. (2007). *Raising awareness of stress at work in developing countries A modern hazard in a traditional working environment.* Geneva: World Health Organization. Available at www.who.int/occupational _health/publications/raisingawarenessofstress.pdf. Accessed October 8, 2021.

International Labour Organization. (2019). *C190 – Violence and Harassment Convention, 2019.* Available at www.ilo.org/dyn/normlex/en/f?p=NOR MLEXPUB:12100:0::NO:12100:P12100_INSTRUMENT_ID:3999810:NO. Accessed September 24, 2021.

International Labour Organization. (2019). *R206 – Violence and Harassment Recommendation, 2019.* Available at www.ilo.org/dyn/normlex/en/f?p=NOR MLEXPUB:12100:0::NO:12100:P12100_ILO_CODE:R206:NO. Accessed September 24, 2021.

Suggested Organizational Shifts to Manage Psychosocial Hazards in the U.S. Workplace

Part III recommends shifts for U.S. organizations to take, based upon the information provided in Part II, to implement measures to manage psychosocial hazards and work-related stress. It also advances an imperative and rationale for occupational health and safety and human resources professionals to collaborate, with the support of top management, to create psychologically healthy and safe workplaces.

DOI: 10.4324/9781003187349-18

Chapter 16

Organizational Readiness
Policies, Planning, and Training

Signaling from the Organization

It is essential for an organization to communicate with the workforce regarding what the organization is doing about psychological health and safety.

Policies

Ensure there is a policy for managing psychosocial risks, whether as part of OHS policy or as a separate policy. Components of effective workplace policies include:

- Written documents with necessary definitions of matters covered in the policy;
- A statement of applicability clearly detailing those who are subject to the policy;
- The policy's goals and measures for achieving those goals;
- Reporting procedures with emphasis on no retaliation for reporting;
- Consequences for violating policies;
- Making all supervisors and employees aware of the policy through posting and repeated and regular training and education, including upon hire;
- Consistent implementation and enforcement;
- Top management's signature on the policy;
- Keeping the policy a live active document—available to discuss and refer to;
- Regular review and updating, such as following a relevant incident and at least annually; and
- Incorporation of and compliance with applicable laws and regulations.

DOI: 10.4324/9781003187349-19

Psychosocial Risk Prevention Policy

The employer should decide whether to have a stand-alone psychosocial risk prevention policy or a policy that sits within the OHS policy.

The organization may want to determine whether there is a need for a separate policy about managing psychosocial risks as well as consider how other policies, such as those originating from the human resources (HR) or corporate social responsibility (CSR) areas, support the OHS policy, in order to achieve common objectives.

> [A policy] related to psychosocial risk can provide direction for implementing and improving management of psychosocial risk within the general OH&S management system. The policy can enable top management and other workers to understand the overall commitment of the organization and how this can affect individual responsibilities.
>
> (ISO, 2021, 5.2)

ISO45003 states that top management should ensure its commitment to preventing ill-health and injuries related to psychosocial risk, and also ensure that promoting wellbeing at work, are included in the OHS policy for the organization (ISO, 2021).

Additional Questions to Ask with Regard to Policy

Further questions to ask include:

- Which psychosocial risks are present in the organization?
- What is their nature, frequency, and severity?
- Has the organization already undertaken certain actions with regard to psychosocial risks?
- Do other policies, such as those in the HR or CSR areas, support the OHS policy to achieve common objectives?

ISO 45003 recommends that the organization should:

- Establish measurable objectives consistent with the policy;
- Develop and implement plans to ensure that these objectives can be achieved (ISO, 2021).

Maximizing the Policy's Effectiveness: Involve Top Management

Involve top management, as well as the HR, OHS, legal, and risk and compliance departments in establishing a policy on psychosocial hazards (PSH) and work-related stress. For greater effectiveness, a policy statement (alone or incorporated as part of another relevant policy) should be signed and endorsed by senior management and should refer to psychological health and safety as it applies to the organization.

ISO 45003 states:

> In establishing an OHS policy for the organization, top management should:
>
> - Ensure that commitments to preventing ill health and injuries related to psychosocial risk and promoting wellbeing at work are included in the OH&S policy;
> - Determine if there is a need for a separate policy about managing psychosocial risk;
> - Consider how other policies (e.g. human resources, corporate social responsibility) support and are consistent with the OH&S policy to achieve common objectives.

Note: As with managing physical risk factors, psychosocial hazards are best addressed with full consultation and the extensive involvement of the workforce. The organization should consult workers and, if applicable, worker representatives, in the development of a policy to manage psychosocial risks. (Consultation with workers is discussed in Chapter 19.)

Keep the Policy a Live Document

Do not have a policy just for the sake of it; do not merely copy an example and attach the organization's name to it. Use it, customize it, do not store it in the back of HR's drawer, and review the policy periodically to ensure it remains appropriate and relevant to the organization.

Planning

A planning process is essential to determine the organization's objectives for the management of psychosocial hazards.

ISO 45003 contains a comprehensive section on planning. Specifically, section 6 sets out steps for the organization to use the planning process to address risks as follows.

> The organization should use the Planning Process to:
>
> a) establish appropriate objectives;
> b) determine how to achieve the objectives for the management of psychosocial risk and fulfil legal requirements and other requirements;

    c) demonstrate a commitment to continual improvement that, where possible, goes beyond fulfilling legal requirements.

During the planning process, the organization should take into account:

    a) the needs and expectations of particular groups of workers (e.g., workers working alone, remote workers, minority groups);

    b) the needs of specific workplaces or sets of operations or work tasks;

    c) the results of the assessment of psychosocial risks, to understand their nature and the underlying causes;

    d) the implementation of actions designed to eliminate psychosocial hazards and reduce the associated risks;

    e) the evaluation of those actions and their outcomes;

    f) the management of the process by reviewing and updating it to meet changing needs, recognizing good practice;

    g) the resources needed;

    h) how to actively involve workers through consultation and participation.

(ISO, 2021, 6)

Canada's National Standard for Psychological Health and Safety in the Workplace also provides comprehensive information on planning (see Chapter 11).

Training Managers and Employees

Training Managers

Managers should be trained and equipped with tools to help them understand the role of workload and PSH. OHS and HR personnel should be trained prior to their training of line managers.

Manager training is essential. Managers hold power, yet they do not always possess the people-management skills necessary to be in a supervisory position. At times, managers may have been promoted on the basis of technical skills and expertise into roles for which they have not been adequately trained. They may also experience pressure from their superiors.

Managers should be trained on psychosocial hazards: what they are, how to identify them, how to manage them, and the resources available to aid them in these tasks.

Training Employees

The organization should set aside dedicated time for training employees rather than adding this training on top of a daily workload. Setting aside time for training signals to employees that the organization views psychological health and safety as an important issue, and that the employees' workload should not be added to for this education. Setting aside time also maximizes employee engagement.

Training Mental Health First Aiders

Mental health first aiders (MHFA) are part of the workplace in Canada, the United Kingdom, Mexico, and Australia.

MHFA-trained employees can aid in helping the organization to:

- Recognize and understand symptoms of mental health problems;
- Provide help to prevent the mental health problem from developing into a more serious state;
- Promote recovery of good mental health by accommodating employees in distress or those recovering from a crisis.

In general, the role of a MHFA in the workplace is to be a point of contact for an employee who is experiencing a mental health issue or emotional distress. This interaction can range from having an initial conversation through to supporting the person to get appropriate help. MHFA are also valuable in providing early intervention help for someone who may be developing a mental health issue.

The Mental Health Commission of Canada has established a learning program called Mental Health First Aid, which teaches people how to help someone who is developing a mental health problem or experiencing a mental health crisis:

> It aims to improve mental health literacy, reduce stigma, and support people with the skills and knowledge to respond confidently and proactively when others experience mental health issues. Just as physical first aid is administered to an injured person before medical treatment can be obtained, [Mental Health First Aid] is provided until appropriate support is found.
>
> (Mental Health Commission of Canada, n.d.)

An organization must communicate to all employees the measures it has put in place to address psychological health and safety. Policies, planning, training, and consulting with workers should all be undertaken according to the psychosocial risks specific to the individual organization.

References and Further Reading

Flourish DX. (2021, October 27). The workplace mental health maturity continuum. Psych Health and Safety Podcast. Available at www.psychhealthan dsafety.com/episodes/bonus-episode-the-workplace-mental-health-maturity-continuum-mBx3dchg. Accessed November 21, 2021.

International Organization for Standardization (2021) ISO 45003: 2021 Occupational Health and Safety Management—Psychological Health and Safety at Work—Guidelines for Managing Psychosocial Risks. Available at www.iso.org/obp/ui/#iso:std:iso:45003:ed-1:v1:en. Accessed October 28, 2021.

Mental Health Commission of Canada (n.d.). *Big picture.* Available at www.mhfa.ca/en/big-picture. Accessed November 17, 2021.

Mental Health Commission of Canada. (2021). *Assembling the pieces: An implementation guide to the National Standard for Psychological Health and Safety in the Workplace.* Available at www.csagroup.org/store-resources/documents/codes-and-standards/SPE-Z1003-Guidebook.pdf. Accessed July 29, 2021.

Chapter 17

Organizational Responsibility versus Workplace Wellbeing

The onus should be on the organization to eliminate workplace risks at source to benefit the organization and workers, rather than on stress management techniques geared to individuals:

> Stress is often a result of work itself, requiring a change to work structures, rather than a shift in the behaviours and attitudes of individuals.
>
> (Asquith, 2020)

More Terminology: Workplace Wellbeing versus Workplace Wellness?

The term "wellness" is not defined or used consistently around the world. Wellness programs are frequently designed to improve the health and wellbeing of employees in order to enhance organizational performance and reduce costs. "Corporate wellbeing," "workplace health promotion," and "health and wellbeing" are among the terms used to refer to workplace wellness initiatives.

Workplace wellness is:

> An organized, employer sponsored program that is designed to support employees (and, sometimes, their families) as they adopt and sustain behaviors that reduce health risks, improve quality of life, enhance personal effectiveness, and benefit the organization's bottom line.
>
> (Berry et al., 2010)

Wellness programs typically address specific behaviors and health risk factors, such as poor nutrition, physical inactivity, obesity, smoking, and stress. Activities aimed at these issues may include biometric screenings, health risk assessments, on-site fitness facilities, group or individual

DOI: 10.4324/9781003187349-20

health challenges, wellness coaching, and healthy foods in cafeterias/vending machines.

Wellness programs and policies may also encompass employee assistance programs (EAPs), occupational safety and health, workers' compensation, and workplace health-promotion approaches.

The ILO states that:

> Workplace wellbeing relates to all aspects of working life, from the quality and safety of the physical environment, to how workers feel about their work, their working environment, the climate at work and work organization. The aim of measures for workplace wellbeing is to complement OSH measures to make sure workers are safe, healthy, satisfied and engaged at work. Workers wellbeing is a key factor in determining an organisation's long-term effectiveness. Many studies show a direct link between productivity levels and the general health and wellbeing of the workforce.
>
> (International Labour Organization, n.d.)

ISO45003-states that wellbeing at work involves "fulfilment of the physical, mental, social and cognitive needs and expectations of a worker related to their work."

Wellbeing at work can also contribute to the quality of life outside of work. It may relate to all aspects of working life, including work organization, social factors at work, work environment, equipment, and hazardous tasks.

Shortcomings of Workplace Wellbeing

By whatever name, the shortcomings of wellbeing measures should be considered. Wellbeing measures are fine, but not if they are used instead of the organization doing the work to prevent damage to employees' psychological health. What matters first is to focus on a healthy psychosocial work environment, then the wellbeing and wellness components can be added.

In relation to workplace wellness, an Australian guide states that:

> It is important you do not adopt a health promotion strategy as an alternative to managing the psychological hazards and risk associated with the work undertaken in your organisation. However, health promotion can work in *conjunction with the systematic approach.*
>
> (Safe Work Australia, 2019)

Workplace wellbeing is not a part of OHS management and should not be confused with occupational health and safety.

It has been common practice for employer organizations to manage OHS programs and policies separately from health-promotion and behavioral health programs that address "wellness" or "wellbeing" (Punnett et al., 2020, p. 227). Organizations should first identify and manage psychosocial hazards that can lead to physical or psychological injury. Workplace wellbeing can then complement OHS measures. OHS might also work with wellbeing programs to raise employees' awareness of work-related stress and measures to improve mental health.

Incorporation of employee wellness measures should be considered with the cautionary note that these programs often place the onus on the employee rather than the employer. The workplace wellness quotes below support this theory.

> Instead of pressuring already-stressed individuals to fix themselves, true wellness requires organization-level interventions.
>
> (Weiss, 2020)

> No volume of training on resilience, mental illness awareness, peer support, mindfulness or gratitude can compensate or make amends for poor work design, issues of overwork, low morale, poor person job fit or things like incivility that are the real factors that undermine people's mental health at work.
>
> (Jones, 2020)

> Training workers how to deal with stress is not the answer ... By focusing on us toughening up, these campaigns deflect attention from the real causes of stress ... While measures to support affected workers are fine, they ignore that stress is often a result of work itself, requiring a change to work structures, rather than a shift in the behaviours and attitudes of individuals
>
> (Asquith, 2020)

> Wellness has long been deployed in lieu of engaging in psychosocial and physical risk management, per every employer's primary duty of care obligations under workplace, health and safety laws.
>
> (Michalak, 2020)

> ... despite the fact that the very best evidence we have about the causes of work stress and burnout point to factors present in the workplace rather than in us, the stress reduction industry and the helping professions focus on individual self-care strategies is at an all-time high.
>
> (Krupka, 2015)

Resilience, mindfulness or other 'stress-busting initiatives aren't the answer to stressful work—while measures to support affected workers are fine, they ignore that stress is often a result of work itself, requiring a change to work structures, rather than a shift in the behaviours and attitudes of individuals.

(Asquith, 2020)

Workplace Wellness in the United States

Wellness in the workplace is an $8 billion industry in the United States, and forward-thinking workplaces may think they are doing a great service by offering yoga, meditation classes, and other wellness services. But the research reveals that those efforts are not working.

A 2019 Harvard Medical School study published in the *Journal of the American Medical Association* shows that workplace wellness programs had no impact on overall health, sleep quality, nutrition choices, health markers, or health care usage, failing to move the needle on the very issues that they claimed to redress. The programs also failed to improve basic workplace metrics such as absenteeism, performance quality, and retention of key employees (Weiss, 2020).

Total Worker Health (TWH), a U.S. program created by the National Institute for Safety and Health that takes an integrated approach to safety, health, and wellbeing, addresses how OHS can help with workplace challenges by calling for organizational interventions rather than personal behavior changes.

TWH recommends the following:

- Recognize links between health conditions that may come from work;
- Listen to workers to find out their challenges;
- Understand that working conditions are a factor—offer more flexibility, such as with start and stop times;
- Get senior level buy-in to culture building;
- Follow through.

TWH also offers that:

A program to reduce work-related stress might

- Implement organizational and management policies that eliminate root causes of stress, such as excess demands or workplace bullying, and that provide workers with increased flexibility and control over their work and schedules.
- Provide training for supervisors on successful approaches and strategies to reduce stressful working conditions.

- Provide training and interventions to build resiliency for stress management and reduction for all workers. Provide access to Employee Assistance Programs.

(NIOSH, 2021)

TWH's program to reduce work-related stress takes the organization's role into account, which is essential.

As shown in the examples below, wellbeing measures taken by the organization are fine, but not if they are used instead of the organization doing the work to prevent damage to employees' psychological health.

- Walmart Canada is partnering with Thrive Global on an employee wellbeing program to offer behaviour-change resources and solutions to Walmart Canada's 100,000 employees (Benefits Canada, January 19, 2021).
- Microsoft Corporation announced temporary "wellbeing days," allowing its employees to take an extra five days of paid leave to ease their stress during the COVID-19 pandemic. The additional paid "wellbeing days" are not a permanent benefit; employees were able to make use of them until December 31, 2021 (Lystra, 2021).
- Amazon has launched an employee health and safety program. Amazon has invested more than $300 million in a program to prevent workplace injuries and provide wellness services to its employees. The aim of the Working Well program is to reduce workplace injury rates by 50 percent by 2025. The program will include physical and mental activities, wellness exercises, and healthy eating support (Esola, 2021).

In summary, the workplace conversation should convey that the role of psychosocial hazards and their possible impacts on mental health in an employees' wellbeing at work is being addressed as an organizational issue, rather than as a problem of individual employees.

References and Further Reading

Asquith, S. (2020). How to resist the "resilience" narrative—and organise for less stressful work. Available at www.tuc.org.uk/blogs/how-resist-resilience-narrative-and-organise-less-stressful-work. Accessed September 18, 2021.

Benefits Canada. (2021, January 19). Walmart partnering with Thrive Global on employee wellbeing program. Available at www.benefitscanada.com/news/walmart-canada-partnering-with-thrive-global-on-employee-wellbeing-program-155858. Accessed July 19, 2021.

Berry, L. L., Mirabito, A. M., & Baun, W. B. (2010, December). What's the hard return on employee wellness programs? *Harvard Business Review*. Available at https://hbr.org/2010/12/whats-the-hard-return-on-employee-wellness-programs. Accessed November 2, 2021.

Esola, L. (2021, May 17). Amazon launches employee health and safety program. *Business Insurance*. Available at www.businessinsurance.com/article/20210 517/NEWS08/912341874/Amazon-launches-employee-health-and-safety-program. Accessed June 2, 2021.

Global Wellness Institute. (2016). The future of wellness at work. Available at https://globalwellnessinstitute.org/industry-research/the-future-of-wellness-at-work. Accessed October 18, 2021.

International Labour Organization. (n.d.). Workplace wellbeing. Available at www.ilo.org/safework/areasofwork/workplace-health-promotion-and-wellbe ing/WCMS_118396/lang--en/index.htm. Accessed November 17, 2021.

International Organization for Standardization (ISO). (2021). *ISO 45003: 2021 Occupational Health and Safety Management—Psychological Health and Safety at Work—Guidelines for Managing Psychosocial Risks*. Available at www.iso.org/obp/ui/#iso:std:iso:45003:ed-1:v1:en. Accessed October 28, 2021.

Jones, K. (2020, December 24). Right information, wrong magazine. *SafetyatWorkBlog*. Available at https://safetyatworkblog.com/2020/12/24. Accessed November 21, 2021.

Krupka, Z. (2015, May 21). No, it's not you: Why "wellness" isn't the answer to overwork. *The Conversation*. Available at https://theconversation.com/no-its-not-you-why-wellness-isnt-the-answer-to-overwork-42124. Accessed November 9, 2021.

Lystra, T. (2021, February 22). Microsoft giving employees paid days off to ease pandemic stress. *Puget Sound Business Journal*. Available at www.bizjournals.com/seattle/news/2021/02/21/microsoft-giving-employees-extra-time-off.html. Accessed February 23, 2021.

Michalak, R. (2020, October 26). Rethinking wellness for law. *Lawyers' Weekly*. Available at www.lawyersweekly.com.au/biglaw/29794-rethinking-wellness-for-law. Accessed November 21, 2021.

National Institute for Occupational Safety and Health (NIOSH). (2021). Hierarchy of controls applied to NIOSH Total Worker Health®. Available at www.cdc.gov/niosh/twh/guidelines.html. Accessed November 21, 2021.

Punnett, L., Cavallari, J. M., Henning, R. A., Nobrega, S., Dugan, A. G., & Cherniack, M. G. (2020). Defining integration' for total worker health: A new proposal. *Annals of Work Exposures and Health*, 64(3), 223–235.

Safe Work Australia. (2019). *Work-related psychosocial safety and health: A systematic approach to meeting your duties—national guidance material*. Available at www.safeworkaustralia.gov.au/system/files/documents/1911/work-related_psychological_health_and_safety_a_systematic_approach_to_meeting_your_duties.pdf. Accessed November 18, 2021.

Weiss, L. (2020, October 20). Burnout from an organizational perspective. *Stanford Social Innovation Review*. Available at https://ssir.org/articles/entry/burnout_from_an_organizational_perspective#. Accessed July 19, 2021.

Chapter 18

Management of Psychosocial Hazards as Part of an Occupational Health and Safety Management System

As discussed in Chapter 4, occupational health and safety (OHS) management systems help organizations to continuously identify and eliminate safety and health risks, reduce incident potential, and implement risk-reducing interventions.

Management of Psychosocial Risks as Part of an OHS Management System

Physical hazards are easier to spot than psychological hazards, but the risk-management process can be used for psychosocial hazards.

> Top management is responsible for the functioning of the occupational health and safety management system and should clarify roles, responsibilities and authorities for managing psychosocial risk in the workplace.
>
> (ISO, 2021, 5.3)

It is important to manage psychosocial risks in a manner consistent with other OHS risks through an OHS management system. Comprehensive OHS management should ensure that psychosocial hazards are assessed and managed in the same way as other OHS risks, keeping in mind that prevention is preferable over remediation.

Measures to prevent psychosocial risks are best implemented on the basis of the traditional risk-management framework. Companies are more successful in preventing psychosocial risks if well-functioning OHS management is already in place (Eurofound, 2014).

Regulations and assessments of psychosocial risks and work-related stress should be part of the management of OHS in the workplace (Lerouge, 2017, pp. v, vi):

DOI: 10.4324/9781003187349-21

"The occupational safety and health profession has a significant contribution to make in preventing the occupational causes of mental ill-health, and is engaged in managing the psychosocial risk of:

- Stress
- Fatigue
- Bullying and harassment
- Violence and aggression."

(IOSH,[1] n.d.)

Psychological Health and Safety as an Integral Part of OHS

Marie Clarke Walker, a safety consultant from Canada who helped negotiate ILO Convention and Recommendation on Violence and Harassment in the World of Work (Convention 190), says:

We look at health and safety as a physical thing, and it's so much more than that. There are a lot more things that employers, governments, can do to ensure that people are healthy and safe ... When we do a lot of our work on workplace health and safety, I think there's such an importance that should be placed on psychological safety ... which encompasses bullying and harassment. It's nice to see the world of work becoming more aware of this and thinking about safety broadly.

(Foulis, 2021)

Research has demonstrated the value of occupational safety and health professionals being directly engaged in and influencing the management of ten different measures, which have been identified as effective in dealing with psychosocial risks:

- Changes to the way work is organized;
- Redesign of the work area;
- Confidential counselling for employees;
- Establishment of conflict resolution procedures;
- Changes to working time arrangements;
- Provision of training;
- Action taken by the establishment if individual employees work excessively long or irregular hours;
- Providing information to employees about psychosocial risks and their effect on health and safety;
- Designating who should be contacted in case of work-related psychosocial problems;

- The use of information or support from external sources on dealing with psychosocial risks at work.

(IOSH, n.d.)

Assessing Risk

In applying standard workplace health and safety principles, risk elimination is the first step; where elimination is not possible, employers should take steps to minimize the risk of psychosocial hazards as far as practicable—for example, by changing the systems of work or the tools used to perform tasks. (Worksafe Victoria, 2021).

As part of the risk assessment process with regard to psychosocial hazards, Australia recommends the following measures:

- *Step 1: Identify psychosocial hazards.* Find out what could cause harm. Consider the main tasks and responsibilities of employees' job and the psychosocial hazards which may be present and the harm and severity of harm that they may cause, including whether the risks are likely and consequences may be less severe and whether the risks are unlikely but consequences may be more severe.
- *Step 2: Assess risks if necessary.* Think about what could go wrong at the workplace and what the consequences could be. Understand the nature of the harm that could be caused by the psychosocial hazards, how serious the harm could be and the likelihood of it happening.
- *Step 3: Control risks.* Consider the effectiveness of existing control measures or implement the most effective control measures that are reasonably practicable in the circumstances and ensure they remain effective over time. Do what can reasonably be done to eliminate or minimize psychological health and safety risks arising in the business.

    Step 4: Monitor. Review hazards and control measures to ensure they are working as planned. Observe if what has been put in place is working and consider whether changes in the workplace might have introduced new risks.

(Safe Work Australia, 2019)

As with managing physical hazards, employers and organizations should prioritize psychosocial risks in order of their seriousness when creating systems to address them as well as prioritizing actions based on the assessment of psychosocial risks.

Account for Organizational Specifics and Particulars

- The list of psychosocial risks must be adapted to the specific organization such as its size, economic sector, work situation, and culture, etc.
- Individual characteristics of workers should be considered when assessing the risks associated with each hazard, particularly in the case of psychosocial factors, since each person may have a different response to stress.
- Input should be solicited concerning the unique needs of diverse populations.
- Particular groups of workers may face additional risks when working in certain environments or under specific conditions or arrangements. To take an example, women tend to report higher levels of anxiety and depression in normal times and in emergencies. They are over-represented in more affected sectors (such as services) and in occupations that are at the front line of dealing with the pandemic (such as nurses). Women often bear the primary responsibilities for unpaid work in the household, including both the provision of care to family members and domestic tasks. On the other side, men, especially if they are expected to provide the family's livelihood, also have vulnerabilities related to any loss of employment.

(ILO, 2020)

In Australia, the employer's duty to exercise due diligence to ensure it meets its WHS obligations includes taking reasonable steps to:

- Acquire and update knowledge of work-related psychological health and safety matters;
- Understand the organisation's operations including any risks related to psychological health and safety;
- Ensure there are appropriate resources and processes to eliminate or manage risks, and these are used to effectively manage risks to psychological health;
- Ensure there are appropriate processes for receiving, monitoring and reviewing information on incidents, hazards and risks, and they are responded to in a timely way;
- Ensure the PCBU has processes for complying with any duties or obligations under WHS laws; and
- Verify resources and processes are provided and used to manage risk.

(Safe Work Australia, 2019)

Cultural Norms

Workplace risk assessments can aid in changing attitudes because they can consider factors such as cultural and social norms that may increase the likelihood of harassment or other interpersonal issues.

Not All Risks Can Be Eliminated

The nursing shortage is a timely example in relation to the global pandemic. Nurses have been forced to work long hours under stressful conditions. In many situations, the organization cannot eliminate the need for longer shifts; however, it can assist in building a culture of support, benefits, and recognition.

The International Labour Organization's (ILO) SOLVE program is a training package focusing on the prevention of psychosocial risks and the promotion of health and wellbeing at work through policy design and action:

> SOLVE advocates that a comprehensive OSH management system should ensure that risk management includes the assessment and control of psychosocial risks to properly manage their impact in the same way as it is done with other hazards and risks, and that health promotion measures are incorporated into the organization's policy.

SOLVE is intended for HR managers, trade unions, employers' associations, OSH professionals, and national institutions responsible for the health and wellbeing of workers (ILO, 2021).

Internal Expertise Not Required: Seeking Assistance from Others

Organizations may choose to use external professionals to assess and manage PSHs, although this is not necessary:

Sally Swingewood, lead standards development manager, BSI and manager for the ISO Technical Committee responsible for OHS management, states that ISO 45003 is very practical and written "very much on the understanding that many organisations have no expertise in this area … The focus in the standard is to manage psychosocial risk by beginning at an organizational level and not an individual level."

Amendments to Denmark's Working Environment Act state:

> If the employer does not have the necessary expertise to handle the safety and health work in the company, the employer must obtain external expert assistance in order to ensure that the employees' working environment is always fully sound.
>
> (Retsinformation, 2020)

Industrial/organization (I-O) psychologists may offer assistance:

- I-O psychologists are professionals concerned with psychological factors that impact employee health and safety in the workplace, most significantly job stress. They research and study human behavior in work settings including conditions of work, work stress systems used to perform work, and how physical and psychological environment affects worker behavior.
- I-O psychologists consult with organizations and conduct research. They typically evaluate how workplace policies are affecting results by conducting evaluations where HR leaders. Organizations may employ I-O psychologists as technical specialists who can diagnose systemic issues and improve human resource practices.

(Spector, 2021)

Many U.S. OHS professionals are unfamiliar with addressing the PSH impacting employees and the work environment. However, it must be recognized in the United States as important and workable to manage psychosocial risks in a manner consistent with other OHS risks through a management system, whether this responsibility is undertaken internally or through the use of external professionals.

Note

1 IOSH is the world's leading chartered professional body for people responsible for safety and health in the workplace, with over 47,000 members in over 130 countries. It sees a valuable role for the occupational safety and health profession.

References and Further Reading

Eurofound. (2014). *Psychosocial risks in Europe: Prevalence and strategies for prevention*. Available at www.eurofound.europa.eu/publications/report/2014/eu-member-states/working-conditions/psychosocial-risks-in-europe-prevalence-and-strategies-for-prevention. Accessed June 15, 2021.

Foulis, M. (2021, July 19). New standard to raise the bar on psychological safety. *Canadian Occupational Safety*. Available at www.thesafetymag.com/ca/topics/psychological-safety/new-standard-to-raise-the-bar-on-psychological-safety/276292?utm_source=GA&utm_medium=20210719&utm_campaign=COSW-Newsletter-20210719&utm_content=A6EBC887-D312-4906-A2F3-B036EDBEAAAA&tu=A6EBC887-D312-4906-A2F3-B036EDBEAAAA. Accessed July 20, 2021.

Foulis, M. (2021, October 22). Psychological safety is an integral part of OHS, says safety expert. *Canadian Occupational Safety*. Available at www.thesa fetymag.com/ca/topics/violence-and-harassment/psychological-safety-is-an-integral-part-of-ohs-says-safety-expert/314156?utm_source=GA&utm_med ium=20211025&utm_campaign=COSW-Newsletter-20211025&utm_cont ent=A6EBC887-D312-4906-A2F3-B036EDBEAAAA&tu=A6EBC887-D312-4906-A2F3-B036EDBEAAAA. Accessed October 25, 2021.

International Labour Organization. (2020). Managing work-related psychosocial risks during the COVID-19 pandemic. Available at www.ilo.org/wcmsp5/gro ups/public/---ed_protect/---protrav/---safework/documents/instructionalmater ial/wcms_748638.pdf. Accessed October 1, 2021.

International Labour Organization. (2021). *The SOLVE Training Package: Integrating Health Promotion into Workplace OSH Policies.* Available at www.ilo.org/safework/info/instr/WCMS_178438/lang--en/index. htm. Accessed June 29, 2021.

IOSH. (n.d.). Psychosocial risks. Available at https://iosh.com/resources-and-research/our-resources/psychosocial-risks. Accessed October 12, 2021.

Lerouge, L. (Ed.). (2017). *Psychosocial risks in labour and social security law.* New York: Springer.

Retsinformation. (2020). Amendments to Denmark's Working Environment Act, 2020. Available at www.retsinformation.dk/eli/lta/2020/674.

Safe Work Australia. (2019). *Work-related psychological health and safety, A systematic approach to meeting your duties—national guidance material.* Available at www.safeworkaustralia.gov.au/system/files/documents/1911/ work-related_psychological_health_and_safety_a_systematic_approach_ to_meeting_your_duties.pdf. Accessed September 22, 2021.

Spector, P. E. (2021, October 19). What is industrial-organizational psych-ology? Paul Spector Industrial and Organizational Psychology blog, Available at https://paulspector.com/what-is-industrial-organizational-psychology. Accessed October 19, 2021.

Worksafe Victoria. (2021). *Preventing and managing work-related Stress,. A guide for employers.* Available at www.worksafe.vic.gov.au/preventing-and-managing-work-related-stress-guide-employers. Accessed September 27, 2021.

Chapter 19

Culture and Climate
Whose Voice Gets Heard?

Organizational Culture and Climate

An organization's culture sets standards and principles that govern decisions and actions within the organization. Company culture, corporate culture, organizational culture, and workplace culture all refer to the same thing: an organization's essence.

> Company culture is reflected in many areas of your organization: your corporate values, your organization's purpose, company mission, the work environment, and employee experience. It incorporates the history, story, vision, beliefs, norms, and expectations held by your company. While company culture is often intangible, it's felt by everyone who interacts with your company: your employees, clients, vendors, stakeholders, and the public.
>
> (O. C. Tanner Institute, 2021)

Organizational climate is complex and dynamic and can affect behavior:

> Organizational climate is the shared belief by employees about acceptable behavior at work. It involves the policies and procedures at work, and reflects the behaviors that are encouraged or discouraged. An organization may have multiple climates, and the exact mix can vary by each employee's job responsibilities. Some of those climates can be complementary and go together, whereas others can be in conflict.
>
> (Spector, 2021)

> Climate would be an aspect of the psychosocial environment of an organization. Psychosocial is a broader concept that focuses on the interpersonal or social aspects of an organization. Part of that is the climate, but psychosocial factors can go beyond climate into other aspects of how people interact.
>
> (Spector, 2021)

DOI: 10.4324/9781003187349-22

Cultural differences in a workplace may arise from different values and ways of thinking of members of a region, nationality, or group in terms of how they approach work, their workplaces, and relating to supervisors and colleagues. Cultural assumptions and biases are often unconscious.

Sometimes certain nationalities may dominate in an organization while other times diverse views may result and play into different accepted behaviors in the workplace and different understandings of what is tolerated. A visible Code of Conduct or policy on Dignity and Respect in the Workplace may be helpful in setting out accepted behavior and consequences for both supervisors and employees.

Countries and workplaces with a very multicultural population and workforce may lead to:

- Different cultures expressing different views on what is offensive and accepted behavior;
- Certain nationalities dominating certain organizations; and
- An employee being bullied based on being part of a minority.

Recognition and Tone

It is important to remember the following when dealing with a workplace culture:

- *Incorporate recognition into workplace culture.* Recognize employees for the work they do, day in and day out. Ensure they have the tools and resources required to get the job done. Communication and recognition can go a long way towards creating a strong organizational culture. Burnout can also be reduced.
- *Be aware of organizational blindness and avoidance.* An organization may allow or give permission to certain behaviors, such as bullying—not always explicitly, but by turning the other cheek. Workers realize this and are coming to expect more accountability from their organization.
- *The tone is set by leaders.* Employees do not really care about the way leaders talk. They care about how leaders behave.
- *Build a high-trust culture.* An employer should acknowledge and manage psychosocial hazards as part of creating an organizational culture of respect.
- *Be aware of working conditions.* Do the company's working conditions show high regard for its employees' health and safety? if employees feel looked after, they will look after the employer.
- *Create positive workplaces.* Front-line supervisors and managers have great control over workers' health and stress; train them to be able to listen and to offer recognition and rewards.

- *Prioritize communication.* Always keep in mind the importance of communication and consulting with workers.
- *Be aware of the power of roles.* Leaders set the tone for a culture and influence behavior.

Employees' Expectations Have Changed: Worker Activism

Given changing employee expectations, perhaps hastened by the pandemic, as well as a focus on racial and social injustice, mere legal compliance is no longer enough.

Worker expectations have changed:

> Surveys indicate that employees in their 20s and 30s want to work for companies whose purpose extends beyond profit-making. They value companies that have a positive impact on society, show a commitment to a diverse and inclusive work force and are focused on issues such as pay equity and the environment.
>
> (Powell, 2020)

The O. C. Tanner Institute's 2021 *Global Culture Report*[1] lays out the state of six essential elements of workplace culture that determine an employee's decisions to engage with and remain at a workplace. They are an employee's sense of purpose, opportunity, success, appreciation, well-being, and leadership (O. C. Tanner Institute, 2021).

The Importance of Psychological Safety When Consulting with Workers

Before consulting with workers, as discussed below, psychological safety should be present in the workplace. "Psychological safety" has a different meaning than "psychological health and safety". Both are important goals for the organization.

Psychological Safety or Psychological Safety Climate

A psychosocial safety climate is the extent to which organizations encourage people to be respectful to one another and create a working environment where workers feel able to express themselves without being criticized or retaliated against.

Amy Edmondson, professor of leadership and management at the Harvard Business School, states that psychological safety and encouraging staff to speak up about any subject is essential for business success. She states that psychological safety describes a workplace where a person feels that their voice is welcome, regardless of whether it they are conveying bad news, questions, concerns, half-baked ideas, or even mistakes (Edmondson, 1999).

The Importance of Communication and Consultation

ISO 45003 states:

> Communication is important because it demonstrates commitment to managing psychosocial risks, promoting wellbeing at work and informing workers and other interested parties of what is expected from them, and what they can expect from the organization.
>
> The organization should communicate to workers and other relevant interested parties' information on psychosocial risk that can be accessed, understood and used. When communicating, the organization should do the following:
>
> - Demonstrate top management commitment to other workers, to increase knowledge and use of processes;
> - Provide opportunities for feedback to top management from workers on actions, programmes and policies intended to facilitate worker involvement;
> - Outline the development of its processes to manage psychosocial risk and their effectiveness;
> - Respond to the ideas and concerns of workers and other interested parties and their input to the OH&S management system with respect to psychosocial risks;
> - Include information on how work-related changes can impact on health, safety and wellbeing at work;
> - Provide information from audits and other evaluations.
>
> Relevant information should be accessible and adapted to the needs of the workers (e.g., in different languages or using different media such as video clips or audio files).
>
> (International Organization for Standardization, 2021, 7.4)

Consulting with Employees

Consulting with employees is a key element of providing a positive psychosocial work environment. Workers' input and participation can improve decision-making about psychological health and safety.

Global support exists for consulting with workers on managing PSH. The U.K. Health and Safety Executive (HSE) states that, as with physical risk factors, psychosocial issues are best addressed with full consultation and involvement of the workforce (HSE, n.d.).

Australia stresses that workers and their representatives should be consulted; workers often know what the issues are and have ideas about how to manage them. Consultation with employees is seen as a

> key part in creating solutions to manage psychosocial hazards, utilising existing health and safety representatives where appropriate and those committees which are independent of senior employees, to encourage communication and consultation within the workplace. Communication is seen to be the centre of any successful risk mitigation plan.
>
> (WorkSafe Victoria, 2021)

Specifically, consultation on psychological health and safety matters in Australia involves the following steps:

- Sharing information on hazards and risks;
- Giving workers a reasonable opportunity to express their views, raise issues, contribute to the decision-making process;
- Taking those views into account, respecting privacy and keeping information confidential when necessary; and
- Advising workers of the outcomes.

Globally, ISO 45003 calls for engaging, empowering, and supporting workers in their roles and responsibilities in terms of managing PSH at work. The employer should determine the resources that employees need and make them available in a timely and efficient manner. Employees should be protected from reprisal when reporting incidents, hazards, risks, and opportunities. The employer should also communicate how all those raising issues of psychosocial risks and concerns will be protected.

The ILO states that to ensure an efficient management of psychosocial risks, workers and their representatives should be involved in the entire process. They should actively participate in the identification of hazards and collaborate in the development and implementation of preventive control measures.

ISO 45003 emphasizes the importance of worker participation. Sally Swingewood, lead standards development manager, BSI and manager for the ISO Technical Committee responsible for OHS management says: "You absolutely have to involve workers in decision making ... leadership needs to visibly commit and set the example" (Foulis, 2021).

Total Worker Health in the United States calls for a participatory approach, with workers having a voice in what the program should look like. Ask and listen to workers rather than guessing what might be best. Listen to workers about needs of their specific workplace.

Collecting Data and Listening: Methods for Consulting Workers

Methods for obtaining data and consulting with workers can vary according to the size of the workplace and the distribution of workers across sites and shifts. Examples include focus groups, worker surveys, WHS committee meetings, team meetings and individual discussions. The choice may depend on the size of the workplace (Safe Work Australia, 2019).

Collecting workers' views may be done using focus groups or small groups (6 to 10 people) from across the organization to help identify common psychological health and safety risks.

Worker surveys, such as People at Work, are another effective tool for consulting workers. When conducting a worker survey, consider the size of the group and organization, how representative the sample will be, and whether individuals can be identified. Information should always be reported at group level to ensure individuals are not identifiable.

If workers are represented by unions or health and safety representatives, it may be advisable to seek their input during the consultation process.

Questionnaires can be adapted to the particular company and participatory methods (meetings with representative workers, observation of work situations, meetings). An advisory group can also be created (FPS Employment, Labour and Social Dialogue, 2020, p. 20).

In today's workplace, recognition of employees' contributions and their voices is increasingly essential to a positive psychosocial environment.

Note

1 The O.C. Tanner Institute assembled and analyzed the perspectives of over 38,000 employees, leaders, HR practitioners, and executives from 21 countries around the world.

References and Further Reading

Asquith, S. (2020). How to resist the "resilience" narrative—and organise for less stressful work. Available at www.tuc.org.uk/blogs/how-resist-resilience-narrative-and-organise-less-stressful-work. Accessed September 18, 2021.

Edmondson, A. (1999). Psychological safety and learning behaviour in work teams. *Administrative Science Quarterly*, 44(2), 350–383.

Foulis, M. (2021, July 19). New standard to raise the bar on psychological safety. *Canadian Occupational Safety*. Available at www.thesafetymag.com/ca/top ics/psychological-safety/new-standard-to-raise-the-bar-on-psychological-saf ety/276292?utm_source=GA&utm_medium=20210719&utm_campaign= COSW-Newsletter-20210719&utm_content=A6EBC887-D312-4906-A2F3- B036EDBEAAAA&tu=A6EBC887-D312-4906-A2F3-B036EDBEAAAA. Accessed July 20, 2021.

FPS Employment, Labour and Social Dialogue. (2020). Guide to the prevention of psychosocial risks at work. Available at https://employment.belgium.be/ sites/default/files/content/publications/PSR_Guide_prevention_EN_2020.pdf. Accessed October 22, 2021.

Health and Safety Executive. (n.d.). What are psychosocial factors? Available at www.hse.gov.uk/msd/mac/psychosocial.htm. Accessed September 19, 2021.

International Labour Organization. (n.d.). Workplace wellbeing. Available at www.ilo.org/global/topics/safety-and-health-at-work/areasofwork/workpl ace-health-promotion-and-wellbeing/WCMS_118396/lang--en/index.htm. Accessed June 7, 2021.

International Organization for Standardization (ISO). (2021). *ISO 45003: 2021 Occupational Health and Safety Management—Psychological Health and Safety at Work—Guidelines for Managing Psychosocial Risks*. Available at www.iso.org/obp/ui/#iso:std:iso:45003:ed-1:v1:en. Accessed October 28, 2021.

O.C. Tanner Institute. (2021). *Global culture report*. Available at www.octanner. com/global-culture-report/2021/executive-summary.html. Accessed September 27, 2021.

Powell, J. (2020, December 31). Bosses: Consider caring a bit—workplace activism is here to stay. You might as well embrace it. *New York Times*. Available at www.nytimes.com/2020/12/31/opinion/work-boss-employee-relat ionship.html?action=click&module=Opinion&pgtype=Homepage. Accessed September 27, 2021.

Safe Work Australia. (2019). *Work-related psychological health and safety: A sys- tematic approach to meeting your duties—national guidance material*. Available at www.safeworkaustralia.gov.au/system/files/documents/1911/work-related_ psychological_health_and_safety_a_systematic_approach_to_meeting_your_ duties.pdf. Accessed September 27, 2021.

Spector, P. E. (2020, November 16). Five proven steps to maximize leadership success. Available at https://paulspector.com/five-proven-steps-to-maximize-lea dership-success. Accessed September 27, 2021.

Spector, P. E. (2021, August 24). Organizational climate is complex and dynamic. Blog post. Available at https://paulspector.com/organizational-climate-is-comp lex-and-dynamic. Accessed November 18, 2021.

WorkSafe Victoria (2021). Preventing and managing work-related stress: A guide for employers. Available at www.worksafe.vic.gov.au/preventing-and-manag ing-work-related-stress-guide-employers. Accessed September 27, 2021.

Chapter 20

COVID-19

Raising the Bar for Organizational Involvement

Psychosocial Hazards Arising from COVID-19

COVID-19 has changed our relationship with work and drawn increasing attention to psychological health at work:

> The pandemic has drastically changed how and where we work, with many people, where possible, working from home, while the conditions for key workers have changed beyond recognition. As we begin to map out the future of the workplace we have the chance to think more broadly about the fair treatment and environment every employee should expect. As people start to return to offices and other workplaces we must be clear that 'building back better' extends to every corner of our lives.
>
> (Government Equalities Office, 2021)

The significant effect that the COVID-19 pandemic has had on many people, both physically and psychologically, has been widely reported.

In the United Kingdom, the Office for National Statistics reports that 19.2 percent of adults are now suffering from some form of depression, up from 9.7 percent pre-pandemic. In Europe as a whole, 62 percent of staff report greater levels of stress, with 81 percent describing themselves as having a "low" or "poor" state of mind, according to a report on mental health and wellbeing in Europe that polled 5,800 people in the United Kingdom, Belgium, France, Germany, Italy, Spain, and Switzerland (AXA, 2020). Globally, the Institute for Fiscal I Studies says 7.2 million more people are suffering from mental health problems "much more than usual."

DOI: 10.4324/9781003187349-23

Expanded Focus on Work–Home Interface

For many, psychosocial risks may have arisen or increased as a result of the COVID-19 crisis. Some of these may have emerged during the period of the rapid spread of the virus and strict isolation measures. Measures such as mandatory work-from-home were widely implemented, resulting in significant changes to work context that may have contributed to work stress for many employees.

Workers working from home were potentially exposed to specific psychosocial risks, such as isolation, longer working hours, and lack of adequate and suitably equipped work areas. It may have become increasingly difficult to leave work at work and home at home. Other stressors may have appeared as businesses reopened their doors and workers returned to their offices. (See Chapter 8 on Ireland's Right to Disconnect and Spain's Remote Work Law.)

Psychosocial Effects Due to Changing Work Arrangements During COVID-19

Ensuring safe and healthy working conditions in home settings can be challenging for employers, as their control over the home working environment may be limited. It is therefore even more crucial now to make sure that workers are involved and cooperate in the implementation of appropriate OSH measures. Innovative strategies and open dialogue between employers and workers are paramount, and employers can support workers remotely by providing them with the right tools and equipment to work from home. It is also important that workers and employers communicate regularly, and that workers are provided with adequate and up-to-date information and guidance materials on OSH, including on ergonomics, psychosocial factors and other OSH-related risks.

(ILO, 2021, p. 29)

Psychosocial Hazards Arising from COVID-19 and Resources for Managing Them

Safe Work Australia's list of work-related psychosocial hazards arising from COVID-19 is comprehensive; it may also be applicable to future infectious disease outbreaks requiring similar implementation of the measures taken during the COVID-19 pandemic.

Safe Work Australia includes the following psychosocial hazards that may arise from COVID-19:

Exposure to physical hazards and poor environmental conditions:

- Concern about exposure to COVID-19 at work;
- Lack of equipment and resources, such as insufficient appropriate personal protective equipment; and
- Being exposed to poor conditions such as cold or noise in temporary workplaces.

Increased work demand and increased workloads:

- Increased time at work, such as additional shifts as production moves 24/7 to meet increased demands;
- Increased workload due to increased cleaning requirements or reduction of workers in workplace due to physical distancing requirements; and

Low support and isolated work:

- Working from home or isolation from others due to physical distancing or isolation requirements;
- Reduction in number of workers at workplace completing physical tasks to maintain physical distancing requirements; and
- Perceived or actual failure of employers to implement new policies and procedure to address changed working arrangements.

Poor workplace relationships:

- Increased risk of workplace bullying, discrimination and harassment as pandemic continues, including towards those that have had COVID-19 or are perceived to be a greater risk to others;
- Deterioration of workplace relationships due to less regular and effective two-way communication; and
- Decreased opportunity for workplace social connections and interactions.

Poor organizational change management:

- Continual restructuring to address the effects of COVID-19 with a corresponding failure to consulting and communicating with workers or provide information and training.

(Safe Work Australia, 2020)

International Labour Organization (ILO) Guide for Managing Work-related Psychosocial Risks During the COVID-19 Pandemic

The ILO's 2020 guide, *Managing Work-related Psychosocial Risks During the COVID-19 Pandemic*, was published to provide employers and managers with key elements to consider when assessing psychosocial risks and implementing preventive measures to protect the health and wellbeing of workers in the context of the COVID-19 pandemic.

The guide considers 10 areas for action at the workplace level that are relevant for the prevention of work-related stress and the promotion of health and wellbeing, applicable to both times of lockdown and in the phases of return to work.

The 10 areas for workplace action to prevent and mitigate psychosocial risks and mental health problems during the COVID-19 pandemic are:

- Environment and equipment;
- Workload, work-pace, and work-schedule;
- Violence and harassment;
- Work–life balance;
- Job security;
- Management leadership;
- Communication, information, and training;
- Health promotion and prevention of negative coping behaviors;
- Social support;
- Psychological support.

For each area, a number of measures are proposed to help address the risks and challenges, including those related to working from home. The measures should be adapted to the specificities of the workplace, taking into account the different sectors and national contexts.

- The guide recommends that to ensure efficient management of psychosocial risks, workers and their representatives should actively participate in the identification of hazards and collaborate in the development and implementation of preventive and control measures.
- The guide also states that the protection of the mental health of workers should be integrated into workplace occupational safety and health-management systems, as well as return-to-work plans developed to respond to the COVID-19 crisis (International Labour Organization, 2020, pp. 6–9).

After COVID-19: Challenges from a Changed World of Work

The COVID-19 pandemic has brought psychological health and well-being to the forefront of employers' awareness in a way that had not occurred previously.

It is uncertain what the post COVID-19 workplace will look like, and it may well depend on the country, state, and individual organization. However, COVID-19 has heightened public awareness and recognition of the importance of health and safety in the workplace, both physical and psychological. This global pandemic has also brought with it an increased consciousness of infectious diseases and the potential for future pandemics, as well as an appreciation of the value of essential workers. As devastating a toll as the pandemic has taken, the urgency for addressing workers' mental health has been brought to the forefront more strongly than ever before.

References and Further Reading

AXA. (2020). *A report on mental health & wellbeing in Europe*. Available at www.axa.com/en/press/publications/A-Report-on-Mental-Health-and-Wellbeing-in-Europe. Accessed 21 November 2021.

Government Equalities Office. (2021). UK's ministerial foreword to the UK's Consultation on Sexual Harassment in the Workplace: Government response, by Rt Hon Elizabeth Truss MP Minister for Women and Equalities. Available at www.gov.uk/government/consultations/consultation-on-sexual-harassment-in-the-workplace/outcome/consultation-on-sexual-harassment-in-the-workplace-government-response. Accessed October 8, 2021.

International Labour Office. (2021). World Day for Safety and Health at Work 2021: Anticipate, prepare and respond to crises—invest now in resilient OSH systems. Available at www.ilo.org/global/topics/safety-and-health-at-work/resources-library/publications/WCMS_780927/lang--en/index.htm. Accessed November 10, 2021.

International Labour Organization. (2020). Managing work-related psychosocial risks during the COVID-19 pandemic. Available at www.ilo.org/wcmsp5/groups/public/---ed_protect/---protrav/---safework/documents/instructionalmaterial/wcms_748638.pdf. Accessed October 1, 2021.

Safe Work Australia. (2020). Mental health. Available at www.safeworkaustralia.gov.au/covid-19-information-workplaces/industry-information/general-industry-information/mental-health#heading--1--tab-tocwhat_causes_psychological_injury?_what_are_psychosocial_hazards? Accessed October 1, 2021.

Chapter 21

Human Sustainability and the Ethical Workplace

Human Sustainability

People are the greatest asset in an organization, and should not be physically or psychologically harmed as a result of doing their job.

Environmental sustainability is very important, but so is human sustainability. In *Dying for a Paycheck*, Jeffrey Pfeffer (2018, p. 3) argues persuasively for the importance of human sustainability in the workplace. He discusses consideration of workplace health and safety issues as a fundamental human right and advances the idea of human sustainability "as creating workplaces where people can thrive and experience physical and mental health, where they can work for years without facing burnout or illness from management practices in the workplace."

Pfeffer continues that if things are to change in terms of workplace well-being, "Employees must understand what constitutes health risks in the work environments, and that includes the psychosocial risks that are today more omnipotent than the risks of physical injury." (Pfeffer, 2018, p 3).

Canada's Guarding Minds@Work, discussing basic human rights and needs, states:

> The psychosocial factors also support certain basic human needs at work … Stated in this manner, the workplace can be seen to have a crucial role in at least protecting, and possibly promoting:
>
> 1. Dignity and respect for the person – the need for a sense of self-worth, self-esteem, and inclusion;
> 2. Security, integrity and autonomy of the person – the need to feel safe both physically and psychologically;
> 3. Organizational justice – the need to feel that one belongs to a community in which there is respect for due process and fair procedures.
>
> (Guarding Minds@Work, n.d.)

DOI: 10.4324/9781003187349-24

Beyond Compliance: The Ethical Case for Managing Psychosocial Hazards

Ethical employers will recognize, integrate, and promote human sustainability. Managing psychosocial hazards and work-related stress is part of this effort.

Complying with laws and regulations does not automatically mean that an organization is operating with fairness, integrity, or safety. The organization should consider a shift away from a compliance-based operation to a human-focused means of operation.

Effective management of psychological health and safety starts with a commitment by those who operate and manage the organization. Along these lines, an ethical employer should abide by the psychological contract. In the workplace, a psychological contract describes the understandings, beliefs, and commitments that exist between an employee and employer. Although it is unwritten and intangible, the psychological contract represents mutual expectations, with fairness and equity important aspects of its operation.

An example of a psychological contract breach might be an employee's perception that their organization has failed to fulfill one or more obligations associated with perceived mutual promises.

The Power of Roles

Robert Chestnut (2020) writes that leaders are increasingly being held accountable for poor behavior and that leadership must embrace integrity. He offers the following six leadership practices:

- Lead by example;
- Make your ethics code your own;
- Talk about it;
- Make sure people know how to report violations;
- Demonstrate the consequences;
- Remember that repetition matters.

Diversity, Equity, Inclusion, Corporate Social Responsibility, and Psychosocial Hazards

Diversity, Equity, and Inclusion (DEI) and PSH

Psychosocial risks may affect workers in different ways, depending on their occupation, their sector of work, and their individual circumstances. "Specific regulations or guidance should be developed to prevent these risks and protect both the physical and mental health of workers" (ILO, 2021, p. 29).

Marginalizing people, and not including and respecting them, puts stress on their wellbeing. Consideration should be given to minorities in the workplace who may be particularly vulnerable to psychosocial hazards because of behavior designed to have, or actually having, the effect of excluding them in some manner.

DEI should be considered in all organizations.[1] DEI and its incorporation into the workplace are an extremely sensitive and important one to leave to experts qualified in this area.

Note: A 2021 international standard, BS ISO 30415, provides guidance on achieving diversity and inclusion (D&I) for organizations of all sizes, sectors and types. It is applicable and scalable to any size of organization. The standard aims to ensure equity, fairness, and equality, and to help organizations embed D&I in their workplaces by providing guidance and methods, including:

- Prerequisites for demonstrating ongoing commitment to D&I;
- Accountabilities and responsibilities for D&I;
- Approaches to valuing diversity and fostering development of an inclusive workplace;
- Identifying D&I objectives, opportunities and risks, actions, measures, outcomes and impacts.

Organizations are encouraged to use a continual improvement plan, do, check, and review approach in order for an organization to achieve D&I objectives (ISO, 2021).

Corporate Social Responsibility

While an organization's board members may not be involved in the day-to-day management of the organization, board members influence the tone and safety culture of a company through the value and focus they place on significant organizational issues and the messages they send to leadership. The board should demonstrate a commitment to organizational health and safety, including psychological health and safety, as an important part of the organization's concerns.

Belgium states:

> A growing number of companies are drawing up charters or Declarations of Principle relating to corporate social responsibility. These declarations concern not only the company's relationships with third parties (customers, subcontractors, suppliers, shareholders etc.) or its environmental policy. Corporate social responsibility also relates to the policy pursued with respect to the company's personnel.

Therefore, particularly when it comes to efficiently preventing PSR, it is very important that such declarations take account not only of this aspect, but also that the messages disseminated outside the company align with the experiences of workers at the company. Discrepancies between what the company proclaims about its personnel policy outside its walls and what actually happens within those walls are a source of suffering for the workers who are then exposed for one or more psychosocial risks. So coherence must be the watchword for companies when it comes to corporate social responsibility!

(FPS Employment, Labour and Social Dialogue, 2016)

Similarly, PSHs should be addressed in the organization's Environmental, Social, and Governance (ESG) policy.

Note

1 DEI is an extremely important subject, but not one I am sufficiently qualified to discuss in this book, despite many years of employment discrimination work for the federal and state governments and being part of international bullying and sexual harassment.

References and Further Reading

Chestnut, R. (2020, July 30). How to build a company that (actually) values integrity. *Harvard Business Review*. Available at https://hbr.org/2020/07/how-to-build-a-company-that-actually-values-integrity. Accessed September 27, 2021.

FPS Employment, Labour and Social Dialogue. (2016). *Guide to the prevention of psychosocial risks at work*. Available at https://employment.belgium.be/sites/default/files/content/publications/PSR_Guide_prevention_EN_2020.pdf. Accessed October 19, 2021.

Guarding Minds@Work. (n.d.) What is psychological health and safety and why is it important? Available at www.guardingmindsatwork.ca/about/about-safety. Accessed July 29, 2021.

International Labour Organization (ILO). (2021, April 28). World OSH Day 2021: Anticipate, prepare and respond to crises—invest now in resilient OSH systems. Available at https://media.businesshumanrights.org/media/documents/wcms_7809271.pdf. Accessed November 10, 2021.

International Standards Organization. (2021). *ISO 30415:2021 Human Resource Management—Diversity and Inclusion*. Available at www.iso.org/standard/71164.html. Accessed October 12, 2021.

Pfeffer, J. (2018). *Dying for a paycheck: How modern management harms employee health and company performance—and what we can do about it.* New York: HarperBusiness.

Chapter 22

Envisioning the Modern Work Environment

A Broadened Focus On and Expanded Thinking About the Work Environment

Psychosocial hazards (PSH) and work-related stress have been acknowledged as global issues affecting all countries, professions, and workers, as well as increasingly being recognized as major challenges to workplace health, safety, and wellbeing. It is anticipated that psychosocial risks will be more pervasive than traditional occupational health and safety (OHS) hazards in future work environments.

> Considering the serious implications of stress at the workplace, organizations need to consider work-related stress and psychosocial risks as part of their safety and health strategy.
>
> (Thye, 2016)

Implementation and Integration of OHS Management Systems as Part of the Overall Management of an Organization

Successful management of PSH calls for a commitment through the organization. Tone and buy-in start at the top, and the importance of commitment by leadership cannot be overstated. Management of psychosocial hazards also benefits from consultation with employees.

Management of psychosocial hazards should be integrated into the organization's broader business processes. There is

> a positive impact of introducing occupational safety and health (OSH) management systems at the organization level, both on the reduction of hazards and risks and on productivity, which is now recognized by governments, employers and workers.
>
> (ILO, 2001)

DOI: 10.4324/9781003187349-25

Time for a Broadened Focus on the U.S. Work Environment

There is a need for a broadened focus and expanded thinking with regard to the psychosocial work environment in the United States. To achieve this, it is important to consider:

- The idea of the work environment as not only the physical place where work is performed but also encompassing organization of work, social relationships, people's wellbeing, and work-related stress;
- Collaboration between OHS and HR to manage psychosocial hazards; and
- Expansion of the range of protection the employer should provide.

The Need to Move Beyond Historical Silos: Build Bridges, Not Silos

OHS, HR, and management should collaborate to address workplace psychological health and safety. A multidisciplinary approach is called for rather than a siloed focus.

Thinking more broadly about the work environment should lead to a focus on collaboration and integration based on bridges, not silos, particularly in terms of OHS and HR professionals. Organizations must realize that the issue of psychological health and wellbeing is multifaceted, calling for a holistic approach that should bring together multidisciplinary teams composed of any or all of the following: HR, OHS, management, legal, ethics and compliance, in conjunction with corporate social responsibility and environmental, social, and governance responsibilities.

Belgium's guide to the prevention of psychosocial risks at work stresses that a very important factor in the success of a prevention policy for psychosocial risks at work is the involvement of all actors at the company, including:

- The responsible person at the company (management board, employer, hierarchical line);
- The head of the HR department;
- The worker and employer representatives;
- The internal prevention advisor for safety, the counsellor;
- The specialist prevention advisor on psychosocial aspects;
- The company doctor;
- Trade union representatives and delegates; and
- The workers.

(FPS Employment, Labour and Social Dialogue, 2016)

Attitudinal Barriers Should Change and Expand

In the U.S. particularly, the intersection of the functions and purpose of OHS and HR should be promoted rather than disregarded. The division in the roles of these professionals should be lessened and more focus should be placed on serving the needs of employees and the organization, rather than on division of roles and job functions:

> The Human Resources and OHS professions have the potential to transform the world of work. Still, this potential will never be realised unless both professions coordinate their efforts, and this will not happen unless institutional egos are shelved ... Especially in the occupational hazards of psychological ill-health, fatigue, excessive workloads, sexual harassment, bullying and more, the HR profession needs to accept the validity of the OHS perspective before working with OHS for sustainable, effective change. It has been easy to describe HR and OHS as two sides of the same coin, implying that they will never collaborate. But we need to look at the coin as a whole.
>
> (Jones, 2021)

Attorney Alena Titterton writes:

> In my experience, neither WHS nor HR professionals are particularly comfortable traversing into each other's disciplines and seem to work to avoid it at all costs ... The difficulty is, ignoring the overlap is simply no longer an option. The complexity in overlapping legislative frameworks is now such that a multidisciplinary approach is non-negotiable for all businesses.
>
> (Jones, 2021)

Kevin Jones notes that:

> The *OHS Professional* magazine for December 2020 contains a very good article about workplace psychological risks and the occupational health and safety (OHS) strategy to prevent mental harm. The only negative is that it is not published in a Human Resources magazine, or one for company directors. The preventative techniques are well known to the OHS profession and based on independent scientific evidence, but it is other managerial disciplines that need to learn the difference between preventing psychological harm and providing symptomatic relief.
>
> (Jones, 2020)

Expanded Focus for OHS

Carlo Caponecchia, Senior Lecturer at the University of New South Wales in Australia, and President of the International Association on Workplace Bullying and Harassment, urges OHS professionals to "go big" to prevent psychological harm:

> Now is the time for OHS professionals to stand up and show that their skills and roles are more relevant than ever. This is not just about supporting people and referring them to EAPs, but it's actually about broader system-wide efforts to redesign how we work … work design affords a bigger, broader and transformative opportunity. This is a chance to finally go beyond mental health awareness, employee assistance programs and individual-level interventions—such as resilience and stress management—to actually create work tasks and structure without sources of harm.
>
> (Jones, 2020)

> The role of occupational safety and health in the future of work will need to evolve to include a more holistic and public health-oriented approach to addressing worker health. Based on a global survey of occupational safety and health professionals, it is anticipated that there will be an increase in complexity of health and safety requirements in the future.
>
> (Schulte, 2020, p. 2)

Carlo Caponecchia and Anne Wyatt (2021) offer a proposed definition of a safe system of work as characterized:

> by an integrated, continually improved set of activities undertaken within a specified work context which together:
>
> - Ensure that work tasks, work environments, and processes are designed such that they are unlikely to result in physical or psychological harm to the relevant stakeholders;
> - Identify and control foreseeable risks to acceptable levels;
> - Minimize harm when it occurs; and
> - Facilitate return to work processes.

This definition includes psychological health within health and safety duties and focuses attention on the fact that preventing and managing psychosocial hazards are a key part of an integrated and comprehensive safety system. The authors state that the proposed definition "seeks to clarify the concept expressed in many general duty clauses around the globe" (Caponecchia & Wyatt, 2021).

What Does a Psychologically Healthy and Safe Workplace Look Like?

Regulations, codes, and standards that have been implemented in numerous countries and globally to manage psychosocial hazards and work-related stress offer a wealth of information to U.S. agencies and organizations on creating a psychologically healthy and safe workplace.

Previous chapters have shown that the EU stresses consideration of the dignity of the worker, while Nordic countries emphasize cooperation between employers and employees, and ISO 45003 encourages top management commitment. Tools from the U.K. Management Standards for Addressing Stress, and Canada's National Standard for Psychological Health and Safety in the Workplace offer comprehensive measures for a workplace to implement psychological health and safety management. Mexico refers to a favorable organizational environment as one in which the employer must carry out actions that promote the sense of belonging of the workers to the organization; its psychosocial hazard-prevention policy is another useful tool.

In accordance with the core principle of OHS as the prevention of harm to workers, the ways in which U.S. organizations regard their workers should encompass ensuring their psychological health and safety as well as their physical health and safety. Although it is time that the U.S. legally recognizes the employer's duty of care as extending to the psychological health and safety of workers, this legislation does not appear to be on the horizon. This shift should then occur by organizational emphasis and message.

Canada's National Standard offers helpful components of a positive psychosocial environment:

- *Balance:* A work environment where there is recognition of the need for employees to be able to manage the demands of work, family and personal life.
- *Civility and respect:* A work environment where employees are respectful and considerate in their interactions with one another, as well as with customers, clients and the public.
- *Clear leadership and expectations:* A work environment where there is effective leadership and support so that employees know what they need to do, have confidence in their leaders and understand impending changes.
- *Engagement:* A work environment where employees feel connected to their work, co-workers and their organization and are motivated to do their job well.

- *Growth and development:* A work environment where employees receive encouragement and support in the development of their interpersonal, emotional and job skills.
- *Involvement and influence:* A work environment where employees are included in discussions about how their work is done and have input into decisions that impact their job.
- *Organizational culture:* A work environment characterized by the shared values of trust, honesty and fairness.
- *Protection of physical safety:* A work environment where management takes appropriate action to address physical hazards in order to protect the psychological health and safety of employees.
- *Psychological competencies and demands:* A work environment where there is good fit between employees' interpersonal and emotional competencies, their job skills and the position they hold.
- *Psychological protection:* A work environment where employees' psychological safety is ensured.
- *Psychological and social support:* A work environment where the organization is supportive of employees' psychological health concerns and provides assistance as needed.
- *Recognition and reward:* A work environment where there is appropriate acknowledgement and appreciation of employees' efforts in a fair and timely manner.
- *Workload management:* A work environment where assigned tasks and responsibilities can be accomplished successfully within the time available.

(Guarding Minds@Work, n.d.)

The Way Forward for U.S. Employers

Responsible U.S. employers must move forward to manage PSH that may result in work-related stress for the health and safety of employees and their work environment.

There is an increased global recognition of the importance of psychological health and safety in impacting lives, work, and wellbeing. The work environment has been shown to affect how people think about their lives and their level of psychological wellbeing.

Effective management of psychological health and safety risks starts with a commitment from those who operate and manage the organization. The success of psychosocial risk management further depends on commitment from all levels and functions of the organization, especially top management.

Organizational leadership must understand the costs of employee ill-health. The toll of unhealthy workplaces is steep, and whether an organization has a positive or negative psychosocial work environment depends on how effectively it manages risk associated with its various dimensions.

Organizations must keep workers safe psychologically as well as physically due to increases in psychological risks at work. It is imperative that workers physical and psychological health and safety are taken into account in today's workplaces, where sensitivities have changed and expectations of the employer and organization are in flux.

Taking a health and safety approach versus a wellness approach leads to a better outcome. Creating a systematic and sustainable approach for psychological health and safety, similar in spirit to how physical health and safety is managed, should be the way forward for the U.S. workplace.

References and Further Reading

Australian Human Rights Commission. (2020). *Respect@Work: Sexual Harassment National Inquiry report, Commissioner's foreword.* Available at https://humanrights.gov.au/our-work/sex-discrimination/publications/resp ectwork-sexual-harassment-national-inquiry-report-2020#PHGSk. Accessed May 13, 2021.

Caponecchia, C. & Wyatt, A. (2021, July 10). Safety and health at work: Defining a "safe system of work." Available at www.sciencedirect.com/science/article/ pii/S2093791121000548?via%3Dihub. Accessed October 6, 2021.

FPS Employment, Labour and Social Dialogue. (2016). *Guide to the prevention of psychosocial risks at work.* Available at https://employment.belgium.be/ sites/default/files/content/publications/PSR_Guide_prevention_EN_2020.pdf. Accessed October 19, 2021.

Guarding Minds@Work, undated. Know the Psychosocial Factors. Available at https://guardingmindsatwork.ca. Accessed November 17, 2021

International Labour Organization (ILO). (2001). *OSH Guidelines on Occupational Health and Safety Management Systems Introduction.* Available at www.ilo.org/wcmsp5/groups/public/---ed_protect/---protrav/---safew ork/documents/normativeinstrument/wcms_107727.pdf. Accessed October 31, 2021.

International Labour Organization. (2001). *OSH Guidelines on Occupational Health and Safety Management Systems.* Available at www.ilo.org/wcmsp5/ groups/public/---ed_protect/---protrav/---safework/documents/normativeins trument/wcms_107727.pdf. Accessed October 31, 2021.

Jones, K. (2020, December 24). Right information, wrong magazine. *SafetyatWorkBlog.* Available at https://safetyatworkblog.com/2020/12/24. Accessed November 21, 2021.

Jones, K. (2021, September 27). Time for a rebrand to organisational health and safety. *SafetyatWorkBlog.* Available at https://safetyatworkblog.com/?s=Time+ for+a+rebrand+. Accessed November 21, 2021.

Mexlaws.com. (2018). Occupational psychosocial risk factors: Identification, analysis and prevention. Available at www.mexlaws.com/STPS/NOM-035-STPS-2018-information.htm. Accessed October 12, 2021.

Pfeffer, J. (2018). *Dying for a paycheck: How modern management harms employee health and company performance—and what we can do about it.* New York: HarperBusiness.

Schulte, P. A. (2020). A global perspective on addressing occupational safety and health hazards in the future of work. *La Medicina del Lavoro*, 111(3), 163–165.

Schulte, P. A. (2020). A global perspective on addressing occupational safety and health hazards in the future of work. *La Medicina del Lavoro*, 111(3), 163–165.

Thye, T. S. L. (2016). Work stress and mental health. *New Straits Times*, April 28. Available at www.nst.com.my/news/2016/04/142074/work-stress-and-mental-health. Accessed October 21, 2021.

Recommended Resources

Podcast

Flourish Dx, 2021–2022. Psych Health and Safety Podcasts. Podcast from Australia with the goal to rapidly advance the practice of psychological health and safety in companies worldwide. Available at www.flourishdx.com/en.

Blogs

Minding the Workplace, The New Workplace Institute Blog, by David Yamada, USA at https://newworkplace.wordpress.com/about/.

Safety at Work Blog by Kevin Jones, Australia at https://safetyatworkblog.com/about-kevin-jones/.

Blog on Industrial and Organizational Psychology by Paul Spector, resources for practitioners, researchers, students and others who consult, research, and study the human side of organizations, USA at https://paulspector.com.

Books and Articles

Duffy, M. & Yamada, D. C. (Eds.). (2018). *Workplace bullying and mobbing in the United States*. New York: Praeger.

Lerouge, L. (Ed.). (2017). *Psychosocial risks in labour and social security law*. New York: Springer.

Pfeffer, J. (2018). *Dying for a paycheck: How modern management harms employee health and company performance—and what we can do about it*. New York: HarperBusiness.

Appendix

Templates for Management of Psychosocial Hazards

This appendix provides tools to manage psychosocial hazards (PSH) through examples and templates from country and global laws and standards. Psychosocial risk-prevention policies, assessments, and questionnaires are included.

Mexico Psychosocial Risk Prevention Policy

Reference Guide IV: Example of A Policy for The Prevention of Psychosocial Risks (The content of the Guide is a complement for the better understanding of this Standard, and is not mandatory)

In this workplace (Company Name) in relation to the prevention of psychosocial risk factors; the prevention of workplace violence, and the promotion of a favorable organizational environment, the following commitments are assumed:

- It is the duty of supervisors, managers and directors to apply this policy and lead by example.
- Acts of workplace violence are not tolerated, as well as any incident that encourages psychosocial risk factors or actions against the favorable organizational environment.
- Measures are applied to prevent psychosocial risk factors; the prevention of workplace violence, and the promotion of a favorable organizational environment, to prevent its adverse consequences.
- A fair care procedure is in place, which does not allow retaliation and avoids abusive or unfounded claims, and which guarantees the confidentiality of the cases.
- Awareness-raising actions, information and training programs are carried out.

- Prevention policies and prevention measures are effectively disseminated.
- All workers participate in establishing and implementing this policy in the workplace.
- The exercise of the rights of the personnel to observe their beliefs or practices or to satisfy their needs related to race, sex, religion, ethnicity or age or any other condition that may give rise to discrimination is respected.
- Spaces for participation and consultation are created, taking into account the ideas of workers and employees.
  (Official Mexican NORMA NOM-035-STPS-2018)

Note: The policy must indicate those responsible (with the capacity to apply it) and the resources available to comply with the policies at all levels of the organization, as well as the assignment of responsibilities to both individuals and work teams, which receive the training for the application of policies.

More information is available at https://dof.gob.mx/nota_detalle.php?codigo=5541828&fecha=23%2F10%2F2018

Canada Free Tools and Resources

Sample Policy Statement

ABC Inc. is committed to the establishment, promotion, maintenance, and continual improvement of a workplace psychological health and safety management system (PHSMS) that:

- Is aligned with our organizational values and ethics and respects the principles of mutual respect, confidentiality and cooperation;
- Has the resources (human and financial) and authority needed to ensure successful establishment, promotion, maintenance, and continual improvement of the PHSMS;
- Ensures a cross-section of employees (including workers/worker representatives) are involved in the development, implementation, and continual improvement of the system;
- Establishes and implements a process to evaluate the effectiveness of the system and implement changes.

Sample Audit Tool

The sample audit tool is an annex of the National Standard of Canada on Psychological Health and Safety in the Workplace. It may be used by organizations to conduct internal audits. This audit tool may be modified to suit the size, nature, and complexity of the organization. The audit tool may also function as a "gap analysis" tool to highlight those areas that require further work to meet the requirements of this Standard. Most organizations that implement this Standard will do so over a period of time.

More information is available at https://wsmh-cms.mediresource.com/wsmh/assets/nu49392rk7k8c48o.

Psychologically Safe Leader Assessment

The *Psychologically Safe Leader Assessment* is a free resource to help workplace leaders evaluate their strategies related to psychological health and safety. More information is available at www.psychologicallysafeleader.com/about/about.

Assembling the Pieces

Assembling the Pieces: An Implementation Guide to the National Standard for Psychological Health and Safety in the Workplace is available at www.csagroup.org/store-resources/documents/codes-and-standards/SPE-Z1003-Guidebook.pdf.

Building the Business Case

The following 20 questions on psychological health and safety may be used for leaders. These questions help review possible exposures to risk or potential for improvement:

1. Is employee psychological health and safety a stated priority in our organizational policy statement?
2. Do people in our organization have a common understanding of a psychologically safe workplace?
3. Is our management team familiar with the legal and regulatory requirements and expectations related to workplace mental health and psychological safety?
4. What is the cost of stress-related illnesses—both physical and mental—to our organization?
5. Is there a system in place to measure the rates of both absenteeism and presenteeism (being unproductive while present at work) in our organization and what percentage of these may be related to psychological health and safety issues?
6. What percentage of disability claims are related in whole or in part to mental health issues or workplace conflict issues?

7. Do our policies align with occupational health and safety, labour law, tort law, contract law, and employment standards with respect to psychological health and safety?

8. Is there a process in place to encourage front-line managers to provide a psychologically safe workplace through such measures as performance indicators and evaluation methods?

9. Are staff whose position includes managing, supervising, or supporting employees adequately trained, skilled, or competent to make good decisions?

10. Do the leaders and management in our organization recognize and respond to conflict in a timely and effective manner?

11. Are the leaders and management in our organization trained to identify the difference between a mental health problem and a performance issue?

12. Does our organization have a policy on work–life balance?

13. Does our organization work to prevent physical, relational, or emotional harassment, bullying, or aggression?

14. Does our organization help prevent discrimination by providing all employees with a basic level of knowledge about mental health issues?

15. Do we have crisis response policies and processes in place for issues such as suicide, violence, threats of violence, or emotional breakdowns at work?

16. Does our organization have a process allowing for open communications between managers, supervisors, and employees that helps us address the needs of co-workers who are traumatized by personal or workplace issues?

17. Do we have a return-to-work policy that considers the emotional, psychological, and interpersonal challenges and allows union/employee representatives to play a role in the return-to-work process including having the opportunity to provide input on the return-to work process?

18. Do we know how to reasonably accommodate workers with a mental health disability at work?

19. What resources in our organization or community exist for employees struggling with mental health issues?

20. Is our organization exposed to complaints concerning the duty to reasonably accommodate persons with mental disabilities, which may include depression or anxiety related disorders?

More information is available at www.thenationalcouncil.org/wp-content/uploads/2019/11/20-Questions-for-Leaders-About-Workplace-Psychological-Health-and-Safety.pdf?daf=375ateTbd56.

United Kingdom

Tackling Work-related Stress Using the Management Standards Approach

This step-by-step workbook is designed to help the organization meet its legal duty to assess the risks to its employees from work-related stress and providing advice and practical guidance pursuant to the management standards approach to tackling work-related stress. Available at www.hse.gov.uk/pubns/wbk01.pdf.)

Stress Policy

The U.K. Health and Safety Executive (HSE) provides an example of a Stress Policy at www.hse.gov.uk/stress/assets/docs/examplepolicy.pdf.

U.K. HSE Managing Risks and Risk Assessment at Work: Risk Assessment Templates and Examples

A risk-assessment template can be used to help keep a record of:

- Who might be harmed;
- What is already being done to control the risks;
- What further action is needed to take to control the risks;
- Who needs to carry out this action;
- When the action is needed by.

The United Kingdom offers examples of risk assessments to show how other businesses have managed risks and as a guide to think about hazards in your business and the steps you need to take to manage the risks.

Examples are provided for the following:

- Office-based business;
- Local shop/newsagent;
- Food preparation and service;
- Motor vehicle repair shop;
- Factory maintenance work;
- Warehouse.

Below is a sample risk assessment for an office-based business:

The company has 18 staff, with one being a wheelchair user. The offices contain a kitchen where staff can make drinks and heat food—there are toilet and washing facilities on each floor. The offices are cleaned every evening by contractors, who store the cleaning chemicals in a locked cupboard. The office block is locked from 9 pm to 6 am Monday to Friday and at the weekends. The building also has 24 hour/7 days a week security cover.

How was the risk assessment done?

The manager followed the advice at www.hse.gov.uk/simple-hea lth-safety/risk.

To identify the hazards, they:

- Walked around the office, noting things that might pose a risk;
- Checked the HSE advice on employees with disabilities:
- Talked to supervisors and staff, including the wheelchair user, to learn from their experience and listen to their concerns;
- Talked to the office cleaning contractors, to make sure the cleaning activities did not pose a risk to office staff;
- Looked at the accident book to see how previous accidents had occurred.

They noted what was already being done to control the risks and recorded any further actions required. They pinned a copy of the findings on a noticeboard in the tearoom *to* encourage staff to help put the actions into practice.

The manager will review the risk assessment whenever there are any significant changes such as new work equipment, work activities or workers.

> (HSE (n.d.), Managing risks and risk assessment at work:
> Risk assessment template and examples. Available at
> www.hse.gov.uk/simple-health-safety/risk/risk-
> assessment-template-and-examples.htm)

The HSE has also published the Management Standards Indicator Tool, a questionnaire with 35 questions for an organization to determine present working conditions and monitor future ones. The tool is available at www.hse.gov.uk/stress/assets/docs/indicatortool.pdf.

The HSE offers more information on Tools and Templates at www.hse. gov.uk/stress/standards/downloads.htm.

Belgium

Psychosocial Risk at Work Alert Indicators

Belgium's *Psychosocial Risk at Work Alert Indicators* tool, updated in June 2020, is used to pre-diagnose psychosocial risks and alert employers to their presence within the company. The psychosocial risk warning indicators can be used in all companies and organizations, regardless of their sector of activity.

The psychosocial risk warning indicators detect the presence of psychosocial risks in the company and to assess the level at which they appear: green light: minor problems. Amber light: warning signal. Red light: alarm.

The psychosocial risk warning indicators can be used in all companies and organizations, regardless of their sector of activity. It invites a participatory approach and the modules that compose it can be completed by a small group of people representative of the company, using the User Guide and the Modules Info Sheets.

Psychosocial Risk at Work Alert Indicators is available at https://emploi.belgique.be/fr/actualites/mise-jour-de-loutil-indicateurs-dalerte-des-risques-psychosociaux-au-travail.

Australia

Safe Work NSW's Code of Practice: Managing Psychosocial hazards at work offers practical guidance for the organization or employer to manage PSH at work. The Code is available at www.safework.nsw.gov.au/__data/assets/pdf_file/0004/983353/Code-of-Practice_Managing-psychosocial-hazards.pdf.

People at Work Tool

The People at Work tool helps create psychologically healthy and safe workplaces; it can be found at www.peopleatwork.gov.au.

International

Copenhagen Psychosocial Questionnaire to Measure Psychosocial Risk

The Copenhagen Psychosocial Questionnaire (OPSOQ) is a questionnaire on psychosocial working conditions, originally developed for use in occupational risk assessment and research on work and health. Three versions of the COPSOQ have been developed by the Psychosocial Department at the National Institute of Occupational Health, Copenhagen, Denmark.

The COPSOQ is a reliable and distinct measure of a wide range of psychosocial dimensions of modern working life. It covers a broad range of domains, including demands at work; work organization and job content; interpersonal relations and leadership; work–individual interface; social capital; offensive behaviors; and health and wellbeing.

COPSOQ III has been used in 40 or more countries. The questionnaire is available free of charge. More information is available at www.copsoq-network.org.

Acknowledgments

A huge thank you and much appreciation to Jeff Moriarty and Gail Sands for providing the opportunity to research this topic for a year and a half as a Visiting Researcher at Bentley University's Hoffman Center for Business Ethics in 2020–2021.

I have a world of other people who I would also like to thank for their work and support: my U.S. workplace bullying colleagues, including Gary Namie, David Yamada, Maureen Duffy, and Loraleigh Keashley; European trailblazers Manal Aziz, Stavroula Leka, and Aditya Jain; Canadian colleagues Linda Crockett and Pat Ferris; Carlo Caponecchia from Australia, and other inspirational people along the way from the APA/NIOSH/SOHP Work Stress and Health Conferences. Thanks too to The Isosceles Group.

The discovery of some excellent books, blogs, and podcasts helped me along the way; they are specified in the recommended resources. Thanks to those authors and podcasters.

Many thanks to Meredith Norwich and Chloe Herbert at Routledge and Faye Gardner at Newgen Publishing UK for all their help, and much appreciation to Susan Jarvis for her excellent editing.

And of course, thanks to my family. Always first.

Index

Printed in the United States
by Baker & Taylor Publisher Services